for the Love *of the* Land II

A cook book to celebrate the British farming community and their food

Compiled by Jenny Jefferies

For the Love of the Land II

©2022 Jenny Jefferies
& Meze Publishing Ltd. All rights reserved

First edition printed in 2022 in the UK

ISBN: 978-1-910863-92-3

Compiled by: Jenny Jefferies

Edited by: Katie Fisher & Phil Turner

Photography by: Paul Gregory, Simon Burt,
Tim Green, Geoff Reardon, Clair Irwin,
Jake Morley, Carl Sukonik, Sam Bowles,
Chris Boyd & Melissa Rodrigues

Designed by: Paul Cocker

PR: Emma Toogood & Lizzy Capps

Contributors: Lis Ellis, Radha Joshi,
Lizzie Morton

Printed by Bell & Bain Ltd, Glasgow

Published by Meze Publishing Limited
Unit 1b, 2 Kelham Square
Kelham Riverside
Sheffield S3 8SD
Web: www.mezepublishing.co.uk
Telephone: 0114 275 7709
Email: info@mezepublishing.co.uk

DEDICATION

This book is dedicated to all the farmers.

ACKNOWLEDGEMENTS

Thank you to Jimmy Doherty and all the farmers;
to The Farm Safety Foundation; to everyone at Meze Publishing:
Phil Turner, Paul Cocker, Katie Fisher, Emma Toogood and Lizzy Capps;
to all the photographers: Paul Gregory, Simon Burt, Tim Green,
Geoff Reardon, Clair Irwin, Jake Morley, Carl Sukonik, Sam Bowles,
Chris Boyd and Melissa Rodrigues; to my lovely friends and to my
wonderful family: John, Heidi and Florence xxx

FOREWORD

BY JIMMY DOHERTY

UK farmers are crucial to keeping our country fed and nourished. They produce high quality, nutritious food and have been doing so for generations. To me, farmers really are the cornerstone of our modern civilisation. It is only from working the land over time that I have gained a real sense of appreciation for the work our farmers do up and down the country.

I have always believed that we must farm in harmony with nature and not against it. This is why regenerative and free-range methods of farming have always been at the heart of everything we do at Jimmy's Farm. Regenerative agriculture is all about the health of the soil and giving back what has been taken out. It helps to replenish waterways, improves biodiversity, protects our wildlife, reverses climate change and preserves our future.

Protecting biodiversity is vital for our future but preserving the diversity of our native rare breed livestock is something I feel equally passionate about. Farming is changing and preserving the genetic diversity of our livestock for future generations is more essential now than ever before. By supporting British rare breeds we are also helping to protect the heritage of our country and its landscape.

Twice a year we hold a wonderful evening called 'The Big Beef Night' to celebrate British beef in all its glory and the star of the show is always one of our rare breed cattle. We talk about how the animals are reared, fed on lush grass and how its beta-carotene gives the fat a fantastic yellow colour, something that would be hard to find in the supermarket! I love to watch diners delight in discovering how you can get the most out of every cut as they watch our butcher work his magic.

Reconnecting with our food and its production is so important and can only be a force for good. The further we are removed from this, the worse it is for the health of our nation.

You too can make a difference by backing British food and farming, supporting local and buying from your local butchers and farm shop whenever you can.

CONTENTS

· ·

PREFACE

· ·

BY JENNY JEFFERIES

For The Love Of The Land II is a small but hopefully solid representation of our agricultural industry to give you at home, wherever you are, a warm welcome into the livelihoods of our amazing British farmers. It offers an important insight into our innovative and inspiring practices, covering sustainability, food provenance, agroforestry, rewilding, community spirit, culture, organic farming, conservation and regenerative agriculture. Our prime objective, though, is producing food. What we can do collectively is eat good quality produce; you only need to cook it and it will speak for itself. It's the rhythm of the seasonal crops and livestock along with a simple style of preparation that allows the food to sing; for one to really enjoy food, one has to know how it's produced.

Whatever diet you choose to live by – whether you are vegetarian, pescatarian, vegan, omnivore, carnivore, flexitarian – we are so lucky to have this luxury of choice, when other people in the world are not so fortunate. We should all embrace and respect each other's choices, be kind, and remember that starvation and food waste is a real problem in the world. A child dies from hunger every 10 seconds. That's nearly half of all deaths in children under the age of 5. There are currently 860 million people in the world who are undernourished and who do not have enough food to eat. 8.4 million people in the UK are struggling too, equivalent to the entire population of London. I'm sharing these rather startling statistics with you because I think it's important to know that not everyone has the same basic needs when it comes to something so simple as food.

The high demand, the supply chain and the ongoing delicate politics are so important, and I think we are all currently on the brink of a food and farming revolution, as global food systems are now at breaking point. We live in an interconnecting world and what affects the UK can affect the world and vice versa. I endeavour to help educate all generations about where our food comes from, and I dearly hope that these books deliver the mighty and heartfelt voices of our farmers in what is clearly becoming a challenging time for British agriculture.

I am so passionate about food, education, independent businesses and people. Home is a good place to start, which is why 10% of my net profits from the sales of For The Love Of The Land II will be donated to the Farm Safety Foundation, which helps to support and prepare the next generation of farmers to be responsible, confident and safe while highlighting the importance of mental health.

Please support your local farmers' markets, farm shops, butchers, fishermen, fishmongers, delicatessens, and bakers, and remember to buy local, buy seasonally, buy sustainably and above all, buy British.

You are a true food hero! Thank you for supporting our mission, and I hope you love the book. Enjoy!

www.jennyjefferies.co.uk

INTRODUCTION

BY STEPHANIE BERKELEY, MANAGER, FARM SAFETY FOUNDATION

The past few years have proved incredibly challenging for the UK's farming industry. There were extreme weather conditions, poor harvests, supply chain shortages and a global pandemic to contend with but, through it all, farming endured as it always does.

A unique combination of diverse soils and temperate climate means that we have some of the best conditions for fruit, vegetables and ornamental crops in the world. We also have some of the highest standards of animal welfare delivered by nearly half a million key workers. Farming affects all of us in our daily lives, even if you might not realise it.

British farmers work for the love of the land. They are a remarkable breed: adaptable, resilient and incredibly hardworking, but their commitment comes at a price. For a workforce that accounts for only 1% of the working population, the industry accounts for nearly a quarter of all fatal workplace injuries, giving it the poorest safety record of any occupation (almost 20 times higher than the GB industry average).

As a charity established in 2014 to preserve and protect the physical and mental wellbeing of the next generation of farmers and farm workers, the Farm Safety Foundation – or Yellow Wellies as many know us – knows that, in this recipe, safety is the prime ingredient. We are working to drive a real cultural change in attitudes and behaviours to risk-taking and poor mental health in the industry and turn this poor safety record around.

We are doing this through the following initiatives:

- Sector-leading research into attitudes and behaviours to understand the risk factors around farm safety and poor mental health.

- Using our evidence to influence policy, practice and change.

- Running campaigns like Farm Safety Week and Mind Your Head to raise awareness, reduce stigma and increase help seeking.

- Delivering high quality training, learning and skills development.

- Working in partnerships with key sector stakeholders, settings and groups to reduce risk taking and poor safety behaviours and provide support.

We are a small charity with a BIG ambition, and we cannot do this alone. We need to encourage farmers to start taking safety seriously, to rethink risk and, importantly, to mind your head.

We are grateful to Jenny for choosing to support us with this second instalment of For the Love of The Land and we look forward to backing British farming by using locally sourced ingredients, grown by our wonderful producers, and creating something truly special.

BADDAFORD FARM & RIVERFORD ORGANIC FARMERS

BY GUY SINGH-WATSON

> *"My enthusiasm for farming has a lot to do with being in nature, and for me that means sharing space rather than controlling and monopolising the countryside."*

When I sold Riverford, the organic veg box scheme I founded some 30 years ago, to the staff (as they were then, now co-owners) in 2018, my plan was to progressively retire over the following years, serenely overseeing the farm on walks with my dog. It hasn't quite worked out that way so far; I am a compulsive entrepreneur and love growing vegetables so Baddaford Farm – the 150-acre site that my wife Geetie and I bought, next door to Riverford's original farm – has turned into a business in itself.

We grow about 30 acres of field-scale produce: lots of strawberries, globe artichokes, purple sprouting broccoli in winter, soft fruits including raspberries, rhubarb, and a few other mostly perennial vegetables, virtually all of which goes into Riverford veg boxes. There are also six or seven diverse micro-businesses on the farm, run by tenants, which produce seeds for gardeners, culinary and medicinal herbs, plants for dying cloth and more. I'm really enjoying quietly facilitating what they do here and having started Riverford on a tiny scale myself, it's refreshing to learn from people who are skilled in their work. That includes our farm manger, Milan, who is the innovator behind our excellent homemade compost among many other things, which I believe is one of the key reasons for our growing success.

My enthusiasm for farming has a lot to do with being in nature, and for me that means sharing space rather than controlling and monopolising the countryside. We recently rolled out an initiative, pioneered at Baddaford, to grow nuts as part of a pasture system – rows of walnut, hazelnut and chestnut trees with animals grazing in between – to obtain food from the land more efficiently and sustainably. We must find a way of feeding ourselves while reducing soil disturbance, and while I love organic farming, our great weakness is over-cultivating the soil. I see the solution as more perennial crops and mixing things up, so you can have produce, grass and wildlife all thriving in the same field. We have an unbelievable population of voles on the farm who could testify to that!

I'm particularly proud of being named BBC's Farmer of the Year twice, as well as Riverford's award for 'ethical product of the decade' from the Observer. I love spending my life this way and feel incredibly lucky to do something so tangibly useful every day. Producing good food, hopefully in an environmentally sensitive way, and being supported by our customers is a real privilege.

WILD GARLIC TARTE SOLEIL

. . . .

A sun-shaped tart to celebrate the glossy, pungent wild garlic foraged each Spring from our woodland. Wild garlic not in season? Simply use spinach or chard instead. For a vegan version, use dairy-free puff pastry, brush with oil instead of egg, and replace the cheese with tapenade or vegan pesto.

100g wild garlic

2 sheets of puff pastry (approx. 300g each)

1 egg, beaten

1½ tbsp Dijon mustard

120g cheddar cheese, grated

60g parmesan, finely grated

Black pepper

1 tsp poppy seeds

Put a kettle of water on to boil. Thoroughly wash the wild garlic and sit it in a heatproof bowl. Pour over the boiling water and leave it for about 30 seconds until it has softened and wilted. Drain and cool it by covering in cold water. Drain it again and then squeeze out as much excess water as you can before roughly chopping it.

Roll each pastry sheet out into a large circle (approximately 26cm in diameter). It's a good idea use a dinner plate as a template to cut around, to give you perfect circles. Put one circle on a lined baking tray and pop the other into the fridge until needed.

Brush some beaten egg in a 1cm border around the edge of the pastry circle on the tray. Smear the inside of the circle evenly with mustard and then scatter over the chopped wild garlic and three quarters of the cheddar and parmesan. Finish with a few turns of black pepper.

Remove the second sheet of pastry from the fridge and place it directly on top of the filling, pressing the edges together to seal. Mark the centre of the circle by pressing the rim of a small glass or cup onto it. This gives you central hub to cut towards.

Take a ruler and lightly score the circle into 24 equal divisions through the centre. Take a large sharp knife and cut each line to the mark you made with the glass rim. This will give you 24 spokes radiating out from a central hub.

One by one, take the end of each spoke and give it a full turn, making two distinct twists in the length. Try and bring the end back down in line with the circle edge. Do this all the way around.

Brush the whole tart with beaten egg, then sprinkle the poppy seeds and remaining cheese over the top. Return it to the fridge for 10 minutes to rest while you preheat your oven to 190°c or Gas Mark 5. Transfer the tart to the oven and bake for 25-30 minutes until golden brown. Serve warm.

PREPARATION TIME: 10 MINUTES | COOKING TIME: 30 MINUTES | SERVES 4

BALCASKIE ESTATE & SCOTLAND THE BREAD

BY ANDREW WHITLEY

"The farming system of a healthier future cries out for honest relationships between producers and consumers."

The task of getting agriculture and food production and processing to 'net zero' is daunting, even for pioneers of the regenerative organic transition such as Balcaskie Estate. It requires that farmers care equally for people and the living world, and at Balcaskie, they do.

The farming system of a healthier future cries out for honest relationships between producers and consumers. The main task of farmers today is to resume their age-old role of nourishing their fellow citizens from nearby fields. It's a scandal that prime agricultural land is ever used for the intensive production of crops that are not even going to feed animals, let alone people. For farmers to flourish while growing less and better, so that we can eat less and better, requires new thinking in everything from plant genetics to economics. Rebuilding trust 'from soil to slice' is Scotland The Bread's mission.

Since 2017, Balcaskie Estate has grown small (by its standards) areas of genetically diverse, long-strawed wheat and rye varieties as part of our action research to find nutrient-dense grains that grow well enough in Scotland and can be skilfully fermented into tasty bread. This isn't about creating another niche market for the well-heeled. In our Flour to the People project (which won the Innovation category at the BBC Food & Farming Awards in 2021), we showed how merely growing and milling better grain isn't enough: it has to be within easy reach of everyone.

Scotland The Bread's modest 'cyclone' mills use very little energy to turn wheat and rye grain into fine wholemeal flour, with almost no wastage. This is important, not just because we are modelling a small-scale, localised route to reducing emissions from food and farming, but because there would be little point in finding, growing and selecting more nutrient-dense grains if we were to damage or deplete key minerals and vitamins while milling those grains into flour or baking them into bread.

Our aim is to re-connect people with the source of their daily bread: where it used to come from, and where it must come from again if we are going to overcome the massive ecological and diet-related problems caused by the current way of doing things. In our Soil to Slice initiative, we share our very special grains with community gardeners, helping to sow and tend them right through to a modest but inspiring harvest of real bread. We also help to upskill community bakers and public cooks so that they too can celebrate and share the healthy produce of those who work the land.

L-R: Andrew Whitley & Sam Parsons (Estate Director) at Balcaskie

SOURDOUGH RYE BREAD

The blue-grey shimmer of head-high rye swaying gracefully in the Fife sunshine as the early September harvest approaches is one of the highlights of the Balcaskie year – perhaps more for the miller and baker than for the farmer, who has to contend with the uncertainties of the weather and a 'non-standard' grain. The 'evolutionary' rye grown at Balcaskie comes from a veteran Swedish plant breeder whose watchword is diversity. Unlike grains bred for intensive 'high-input' systems, Hans Larsson's rye is an evolving population of many different strains with the ability to adapt to varied micro-climates and soils while needing no chemical nasties to cope with pests and diseases.

Sourdough rye bread is one of the easiest, tastiest and most digestible breads in the world. If you haven't got a sourdough 'starter' on the go, it's easy to make one from organic rye flour and water, but it does take four or five days to establish a stable fermentation. You can order an authentic Bread Matters rye sourdough culture, as well as books with the essential know-how, from the Scotland The Bread website (scotlandthebread.org).

For the production sourdough

80g sourdough starter (from the fridge)

250g wholemeal rye flour (such as Scotland The Bread 'Evo Rye' flour)

420g water at 40°c

For the final dough

650g production sourdough*

320g wholemeal rye flour

7g sea salt

For the production sourdough

Mix all the ingredients together thoroughly (with your hand, ideally), then cover and leave to ferment in a warm place for 24 hours.

For the final dough

*There should be a wee bit of the production sourdough left over; keep it in the fridge for your next bake.

Mix all the ingredients together and then shape the dough with a little water on your hands and the worktop. This should produce a consistency that is firm enough to control the final rise and allow acidity to develop.

Prove the dough at room temperature (not too warm) for 3-5 hours (maybe a bit longer if your starter is young). Turn on your oven about 30 minutes before you reckon the dough is fully risen.

Bake the loaf at 210°c for about 40 minutes. Try to leave it for a day before cutting thinly; the flavour will develop and the bread should be a little less sticky and even more digestible.

PREPARATION TIME: 2 DAYS | COOKING TIME: 40 MINUTES | MAKES 1 LOAF

BELVOIR FARM LTD

BY PEV MANNERS

"We have always tried to look after nature on our farm. Dad and I have planted about 10,000 trees in the last 70 years on the farm and we continue doing so today."

My father started Belvoir Fruit Farms in the late 1970s as a diversification from our arable farm with a pick-your-own, here at Belvoir in Leicestershire. The fruit farm was not successful so in 1984 he was looking for new ideas, and while thinking about making a pressed strawberry drink from the abundance of over-ripe strawberries on the farm he went home and found Mum making her elderflower cordial. After hand-filling some 30 bottles together, mostly to give to appreciative friends, they decided to make 100 cases and try to sell them; the drinks business was born. Dad sold them to delicatessens and farm shops from the back of his battered Mercedes and to his surprise they called back for more.

Today, we are still making Mum's elderflower cordial to the same recipe. I joined in 1992 and took over the business on Dad's retirement. Since then, we have slowly grown as people discovered our natural, delicious drinks and now we sell widely across the UK and export to 30 different markets worldwide. We now make c.20m bottles in total at our new factory, which was purpose-built by extending two old grain stores on the farm.

Our range has grown too and we now make lots of different cordials, sparkling drinks and rich punches. We renamed the business Belvoir Farm Drinks in 2020 because we no longer grow fruit, but all our drinks are made from masses of fruits, flowers and spices: real kitchen cupboard ingredients for the very best natural taste. We use no artificial colours, flavours, sweeteners or preservatives and the taste of our drinks comes from real proper ingredients. That's why we call them 'Crafted with Nature'.

We have always tried to look after nature on our farm. Dad and I have planted about 10,000 trees in the last 70 years on the farm and we continue doing so today. Two years ago, we planted 1,500 elder trees and 2,500 English hardwood trees. We are part of the Countryside Stewardship scheme and have 60 acres of organic elder plantations, owl boxes, beehives and fields of wild bird seed mix. We also feed over-wintering birds and grow willow for wood-chip power-plants, as well as planning more woodland planting in the near future. In the factory, we are proud to have a set of clear sustainability goals: we have achieved zero waste to landfill and recycle all our waste streams, we are c.25% solar powered by our own PV roof and all our waste streams are audited by Certified Sustainable.

LEMON AND ELDERFLOWER DRIZZLE CAKE

Nestled away in the Leicester countryside, our 60 acres of organic elderflower burst into bloom for just 6 weeks each year. Handpicked by the local community and brought to our doorstep, the fragrant flowers are carefully crafted into delicious Elderflower Cordial: the perfect ingredient for an extra special drizzle cake.

For the cake

225g (8oz) soft margarine or butter

225g (8oz) caster sugar

1 lemon, zested and juiced

4 large eggs

225g (8oz) self-raising flour

2 tbsp hot water

For the drizzle

100ml (4fl oz) Belvoir Elderflower Cordial

Sprinkle of granulated sugar

For the cake

Preheat the oven to 180°c/160°c fan/Gas Mark 4. Grease a 20cm round, deep, loose-bottomed tin and line with baking parchment.

Place the butter, sugar and lemon zest in a large bowl. Use an electric whisk to beat this mixture until pale and fluffy. Gradually add the eggs, whisking well between additions and adding 2 tablespoons of the flour with the last egg to prevent curdling.

Sift over the remaining flour, then gently fold in with a metal spoon along with the hot water. Spoon the cake batter into the prepared tin, level the surface and bake in the preheated oven for 45-50 minutes, or until it is shrinking away from the sides of the tin. A fine skewer inserted in the centre should come out clean. Let the cake cool in the tin for 5 minutes.

For the drizzle

Sieve the lemon juice into a small jug to remove the bits, then stir in the cordial. Use a fine skewer to prick the warm cake all over. Pour over the lemony elderflower syrup, then sprinkle over the sugar. It should sink in but leave a crunchy crust. Leave to cool completely before removing the cake from the tin, then serve in wedges.

PREPARATION TIME: 15 MINUTES | COOKING TIME: 45-50 MINUTES | SERVES 12

THE BUFFALO FARM

BY STEVEN MITCHELL

"In July 2021, thanks to the support of our customers and a very successful crowdfunding scheme, we were able to make a £2m investment to create Scotland's first ever Buffalo Dairy and are proud to be the first producers of Scottish buffalo mozzarella and buffalo ice cream."

The Buffalo Farm has Scotland's largest herd of water buffalo and was set up by Steve Mitchell in the spring of 2005. Steve is very proud to be following in the footsteps of Robert Mitchell who began farming in Fife in the early 1800s. We have developed several routes to market from the early days of traditional farmers' markets to a well-established farm shop and café, milk bar and online butchery, all of which are serviced from our own in-house butchery at Boglily Steading.

We have received tremendous media interest over the years with Steve appearing on a range of food and farming programs; The F Word with Gordon Ramsay and two series of This Farming Life are particular highlights. We have also picked up a host of awards from Scotland Food and Drink including Meat Product of the Year, several Great Taste Awards, and in 2021 we were crowned UK's Best Butchers at the Great British Food Awards.

Steve was attracted to buffalo due to their versatility (he secretly also loved the fact that they are very similar to his beloved cows!) and the benefits are countless; they produce a very healthy meat that is lower in cholesterol, higher in mineral content and contains less than half the total fat content of conventional lean beef. The milk has almost double the butter fat than conventional cow's milk and is a great mineral source, but crucially contains much less cholesterol.

In July 2021, thanks to the support of our customers and a very successful crowdfunding scheme, we were able to make a £2m investment to create Scotland's first ever Buffalo Dairy and are proud to be the first producers of Scottish buffalo mozzarella and buffalo ice cream. We wanted to create a product that put Scotland on the map and could be considered world-class. Mozzarella is what buffalo milk has been famous for, but we are really excited by the diverse opportunities that this milk gives us. Our ice cream has already become a huge hit with our customers, while Steve and the team are excited about getting to work on other products in the not-too-distant future.

A simple recipe for success is our healthy happy animals, our team, and our customers: without any of these ingredients, the business would not be what it is today.

BELLO BUFFALO LASAGNE

· ·

This is a dish for autumnal comfort eating on a grand scale. Rich, hearty and restorative, it showcases the versatility and tastiness of buffalo in spectacular style. The secret is long, slow cooking at the beginning to ensure maximum flavour at the end. It's worth the time, trust me.

For the ragu

Extra virgin olive oil

1 large onion, diced

2 sticks of celery, diced

2 carrots, diced

4 cloves of garlic, finely chopped

500g buffalo mince

400g tinned chopped tomatoes

400g tomato passata

4 sprigs of thyme, leaves only

Small bunch of basil, leaves only

Salt and pepper, to taste

For the cheese sauce

50g butter

50g plain flour

750ml full-fat milk

1 tsp English mustard

50g good mature cheddar, grated

50g parmesan, grated

To assemble

9-10 sheets of fresh or dried lasagne

100g good mature cheddar, grated

250g buffalo mozzarella, sliced

For the ragu

Heat a good glug of extra virgin olive oil on a medium-high heat in a large, heavy-based frying pan. Add the onion, celery, carrot and garlic to the pan and cook until the onion is softened and translucent. Break up the buffalo mince, add it to the pan and brown all over. Add the tinned tomatoes, passata and herbs, stir well and season to taste. Bring the ragu to the boil then turn the heat right down and simmer at a gentle blip for 1 hour 30 minutes.

For the cheese sauce

Melt the butter on a medium heat in a medium saucepan and add the flour all at once, whisking vigorously. Heat for 1 minute, then whisk in the milk bit by bit. Don't be alarmed if it starts to look lumpy: it will be velvety smooth very shortly, just keep whisking. Once the sauce has thickened, add the mustard, cheddar and parmesan before seasoning to taste with salt and pepper.

To assemble

Preheat your oven to 200°c/180°c fan/Gas Mark 6. Put about a third of the ragu in the base of a rectangular ovenproof dish that holds around 4 pints (or measures roughly 30 by 20 by 8cm). Spoon one third of the white sauce on top and arrange a layer of lasagne sheets on top of that. It doesn't matter if they overlap a bit.

Spoon half of the remaining meat sauce on top, then half of the white sauce over that and arrange another layer of lasagne sheets on top. Add the remaining ragu and remaining white sauce. Sprinkle over the cheddar cheese and place the buffalo mozzarella slices on top. If you're using dried lasagne, leave the assembled lasagne to sit for an hour before it goes in the oven so the pasta softens a bit.

Finish with a good grind of black pepper on top and cook in the middle of the preheated oven for 40 minutes, until golden brown on top and preferably slightly overflowing because it looks lovely that way. Serve with a simple garlic bread, it really doesn't need anything else!

THE BULL INN

BY GEETIE SINGH-WATSON

"Our passion is trying to engage people with seasonal field-grown produce because ultimately, a vegetable grown in this way is going to taste the very best it can."

I opened the Bull Organic Inn in December 2019, with chef Johnny Tilbrook and manager Philippa Hughes at the helm. Four months later we were closed for Covid. But all was not lost. By the end of the year, we had The Times' Eco Hotel of 2020 award, and were recommended by Sawdays and National Geographic for food. We were thrilled! And the accolades have continued to roll in. Johnny and Philippa run the business with skill and finesse which brings endless praise from customers and makes me incredibly proud.

Our purpose is to prove that a delicious meal and a luxurious stay in a hotel can be done with a much smaller ecological footprint, sometimes even a positive one. Our passion is trying to engage people with seasonal field-grown produce because ultimately, a vegetable grown in this way is going to taste the very best it can — we'd be foolish not to let our menus be led by this. Much of the veg we use is field-grown on our own farm, Baddaford, which is run by my husband Guy. We're in the early stages of forming relationships with more small suppliers to facilitate this approach to our food, from a Cornish family business that's trailblazing sustainable fishing to local farms and wholesalers.

We operate in a very instinctive closed loop at the inn, embracing the whole of each ingredient whether that's a fish, a beast or a vegetable. Our chefs do the butchering, utilising everything from the limited prime cuts to the bones and trimmings. Portions are carefully managed to avoid waste from the plate, which is also a healthier approach than leaving our diners uncomfortably full. We keep our dishes simple, our beer local and our wines European – all organic of course – with a mindset that sees every ingredient as valuable. Sometimes we do have to compromise on our values, and we are open about that: we call it the Conscious Compromise. Being honest about what business does is essential. We love it and it's fun, not worthy, plus the food is delicious!

I have always been obsessed with farming and grew up surrounded by farms in Herefordshire where my mum taught me to respect these stewards of the land. The ability they have to maintain our wildlife, our planet and our food is a very special thing. I feel really lucky to have married such a wonderful organic farmer myself who shares my ethos and is so committed to doing what he loves, just as I am and will always be.

ROASTED CAULIFLOWER WITH POTATO PURÉE, HAZELNUT PICADA, RAINBOW CHARD AND GOAT'S CURD

· ·

This recipe came about because at The Bull Inn we believe in making vegetables a standout in any dish. We wanted to take the humble cauliflower and show people that you can do much more with it than just cauliflower cheese (even if delicious!) as demonstrated in this delicious dish.

For the purée

4 large potatoes (around 800-900g)

800ml full-fat milk

4 cloves of garlic

1 bay leaf

300g hazelnuts

3 lemons, juiced (around 75ml)

150ml olive oil

For the picada

1 red chilli, deseeded

1 clove of garlic

2½ tbsp olive oil

2 tsp sherry vinegar

Good pinch of sea salt flakes

To finish

2 large cauliflowers

Sprig of thyme

Knob of butter

Salt and pepper

100g rainbow chard

100g goat's curd

Start with your potato and hazelnut purée. Peel and wash the potatoes, cut them into small chunks and place in a saucepan with the milk, garlic cloves and bay leaf. Bring to a simmer and cook until the potatoes are soft. Meanwhile, toast the hazelnuts in the oven at 180°c until golden (4-6 minutes should be about right). Allow them to cool and then use a tea towel to rub the skins off. Take 250g of your toasted hazelnuts, reserving the rest for the picada, and blend or crush them with a rolling pin into a fine powder. Make sure the hazelnuts are completely cool before doing this, as if they are still warm you will release the natural oils and make a paste rather than a powder.

Once cooked, drain the potatoes and reserve the infused milk, discarding the bay leaf. Put the potatoes and garlic back into the pan with the lemon juice and olive oil, then add the warm milk a little at a time while using a stick blender to create a nice smooth purée. Use a spoon to fold the hazelnut powder through the purée, giving it a nice nutty texture, then add salt and pepper to taste. Set aside to reheat later.

For the picada, chop the remaining 50g of toasted hazelnuts into a chunky texture. Finely dice the chilli and garlic, then combine these and the hazelnuts with the olive oil, sherry vinegar and salt. Mix well and set aside.

Preheat your oven to 200°c. Cut the cauliflower into large florets, then halve each one so there is a flat side. Pan fry the florets cut side down in a smoking hot ovenproof frying pan with a splash of sunflower oil, until they have a nice caramelisation. Flip the florets over, add the thyme and butter, season with salt to taste and then finish in the preheated oven for about 8 minutes, so that the cauliflower retains some bite.

Meanwhile, reheat your potato purée and gently wilt the chard in a pan with a knob of butter, splash of lemon juice, salt and pepper to taste.

To serve, assemble all the elements on your plate with the purée on the bottom followed by the roasted cauliflower and wilted chard, finished with generous amounts of the picada and goat's curd.

PREPARATION TIME: 30 MINUTES | COOKING TIME: 30 MINUTES | SERVES 4

CLOUGHER FARM

BY VICTOR CHESTNUTT

"What's encouraging to see though is the reconnection to local food that people have found during the Covid-19 pandemic, and the way that manifests in more country markets and even dairy vending machines to serve rural areas with quality local produce."

I'm a sixth-generation farmer in North Antrim, Northern Ireland, about 5 miles from the Giant's Causeway where my family have long worked the land. Farming is in my blood; I started young and went on to breed pedigree Texel sheep which became very successful and have won numerous awards. My involvement with Texels has taken me to shows all over the UK, from Caithness to Cornwall, and even to South Brazil as a judge. We also breed Charolais, Aberdeen Angus and British Blue beef cattle on the farm, where I work alongside my wife Carol and our son David, who runs his own dairy business on-site. We also have a daughter, Zara, who works in the agri-food sector.

I'm proud to farm an area that punches well above its weight for food production; farmers in Northern Ireland produce food for over 10 million people even though the population is around 1.6 million. Farming is a huge part of our economy and we must protect that, as well as the many thousands of livelihoods involved in the agri-food industry. My involvement with the Ulster Farmers' Union (UFU) came from a desire to help other farmers.

Farming is my life, but the UFU has given me a taste for agri-politics too because I'm very passionate about representing Northern Ireland's farmers to the public. I was elected Deputy in 2016 and then President in 2020 to April 2022, during which time the job has grown thanks to the difficulties of Brexit, with three parliaments to liaise with and many ongoing issues to manage. What's encouraging to see though is the reconnection to local food that people have found during the Covid-19 pandemic, and the way that manifests in more country markets and even dairy vending machines to serve rural areas with quality local produce.

When it comes to food, I like to see what I'm eating on the plate – no fuss and frills, just quality – and this starts with great livestock, grazed in Northern Ireland on some of the best grass in the world. Our cattle are treated as individuals on the smaller scale farms here, and I believe there's a way to farm sensitively that does good for the environment, the local economy and the people who love this way of life.

SIRLOIN STEAKS WITH BALSAMIC ROASTED VEG

· ·

I've chosen beefandlambni.com's sirloin steaks with balsamic roasted veg recipe, because it's a great representation of the high-quality food that Northern Ireland farmers produce to world-leading standards. It's a delicious, easy meal that has an abundance of nutrients that are required to help us stay healthy.

1 yellow pepper

1 orange pepper

2 red onions

2 courgettes

25g cherry tomatoes

1 clove of garlic

1 lemon

3 tbsp olive oil

1 tbsp balsamic vinegar

2 medium Northern Ireland Farm Quality Assured sirloin steaks

Salt and pepper

Preheat the oven to 180°c or Gas Mark 6. Meanwhile, deseed the peppers and cut into wedges, peel the onions and cut into wedges, slice the courgettes into rounds and cut the cherry tomatoes into wedges. Place all the prepared veg except the courgette on a baking tray.

Peel and crush the garlic, juice the lemon and then mix them with 2 tablespoons of the olive oil. Drizzle this over the vegetables, toss to coat and spread out in an even layer.

Roast the vegetables in the preheated oven for 20 minutes, then remove the tray and add the courgettes along with the remaining olive oil. Roast for a further 15 minutes, drizzle over the balsamic vinegar and then roast the veg for a final 5 minutes.

When the veg is almost done, brush the steaks with a little olive oil and season with black pepper. Heat a large frying pan over a high heat. When the pan is very hot, add the steaks and cook until done to your preference, according to the following timings:

2 minutes on each side for medium-rare

3 minutes on each side for medium

4 minutes on each side for medium well

5 minutes on each side for well done

Transfer the cooked steaks to a plate, then allow them to rest before seasoning to taste and serving with the balsamic roasted vegetables.

(Recipe from www.beefandlambni.com)

PREPARATION TIME: 10 MINUTES | COOKING TIME: 40 MINUTES | SERVES 2

COLWITH FARM

· ·

BY CHRIS DUSTOW

"Clare and I also have three young children showing interests in farming and the farm shop, who give us all an extra incentive to keep working so hard."

Here at Colwith Farm we are passionate about producing premium quality potatoes. Based in the heart of Cornwall, our fifth-generation business is big on sustainability and doing all we can to look after the environment for our future generations. My family have been farming Colwith for just shy of 90 years and have always grown potatoes but also, like most farms, had a mixed bag of beef, sheep, pigs, dairy cows and cereals. In the last 10 years we have decided to specialise more by growing predominantly potatoes, cereals and creating a farm shop.

Today the farm has a fantastic team of around 15 dedicated staff who help to keep all the wheels turning. They include myself, the farm manager; my wife Clare who looks after compliance, accounts and our staff; my dad Michael who looks after crop health; and my grandad Clive who is 90 years old now and retired, but still loves to be involved. My brother Steve created the on-site Colwith Farm Distillery, where he produces premium award-winning spirits by making alcohol from our potatoes. Clare and I also have three young children showing interests in farming and the farm shop, who give us all an extra incentive to keep working so hard.

At Colwith we have a unique range of potato products available which allows us to sell to a vast array of customers and a variety of markets. We produce our own fresh chips on site, sell direct to fish and chip shops, and supply some of Cornwall's best pasty companies, merchants and wholesalers as well as Colwith Farm Distillery and various crisp companies. We have also secured long term contracts locally, which helps us reinvest into our potato packing and storage facilities as we did in 2020 by putting 700k into modernising our nine-year-old setup.

In 2019 we won Family Farming Business of the Year from the Farmers Guardian, which was a huge accolade for us on a national level. In 2021 we won Commercial Farmer of the Year from the Cornwall Farm Business Awards, and in the same year our farm shop also won the Duke of Cornwall's award. On my brother's side of the business, Colwith Farm Distillery has scooped 'best in the world' for their Aval Dor Vodka two years running now. We are so proud of what he has achieved and look forward to more exciting developments and diversifications for our future.

FOR THE LOVE OF THE LAND II

· ·

PAGE 48

BREAKFAST POTATOES

. . . .

Potatoes can be eaten at any meal, but they make a great breakfast to set you off right for the day. This tasty dish is great as a side with British sausages and hearty enough to eat on its own too.

1kg Maris Pipers (or other floury potatoes)

1.5 litres chicken stock

1 tsp fine salt

6 rashers of bacon, finely diced

1 medium onion, finely diced

1 clove of garlic, finely diced

120ml vegetable oil

Sea salt and black pepper, to taste

1 tbsp fresh finely chopped parsley

Peel the potatoes, then dice them into bite-size (approximately 2cm) cubes. Place the potatoes in a large pan and pour in the chicken stock, which should be enough to comfortably cover them. Add the fine salt, then bring to the boil and cook until just about tender when tested with a knife. It's important not to overcook them at this stage.

Drain the potatoes (but don't rinse them) and then leave in the colander to steam dry, preferably until they stop steaming completely, but a minimum of 5 minutes will work. Shake the colander to roughen up the edges on the potatoes.

In a large frying pan on a medium heat, fry the diced bacon until it begins to get crisp. Add the diced onion and continue frying until it starts to soften and lightly brown. Stir in the garlic and fry for 1-2 more minutes, then transfer the bacon mixture to a bowl.

Pour the vegetable oil into the same pan you used to cook the bacon and place on a high heat. When the oil is nice and hot, carefully add the potatoes. Fry while tossing somewhat frequently until they are a deep golden colour and crispy on the outside. This can take 15 minutes or more.

When the potatoes are ready, discard the excess oil, then add the bacon mixture back to the pan and stir gently until heated through. Season to taste with sea salt, black pepper and fresh parsley then serve up and enjoy!

PREPARATION TIME: 10 MINUTES | COOKING TIME: 25 MINUTES | SERVES 4

DROITWICH SALT

BY GILLIAN KERTON

"The Droitwich brine salt springs are estimated to be approximately 200 million years old and are thought to be one of the purest in the world! This 100% natural product is sourced from the pumproom less than 3 miles away from the Saltworks on our farm."

As a fifth-generation farming family, my husband Will and I both grew up in Droitwich and are passionate about our relationship with the land. We are members of the Mid Tier Countryside Stewardship Scheme which includes planting crops to feed birds in winter, new hedgerows and wildflower meadows. We also now farm extensively, replicating methods from 50 to 100 years ago that work with the land. Originally a dairy farm which my late father and I diversified into award-winning ice cream, the pressures of our sector continually push us to diversify our business. Today we only have a small beef herd and use a neighbouring farm's milk for our ice cream, both of which feature strongly in our farm café and family farm events.

We started our journey reviving historic Droitwich Salt in 2016 as we'd been smitten with the story and quality of this local natural resource. What's not to love about a product that put Droitwich on the map (the salt springs were the reason the Romans came to the area!) and also has incredible purity, taste and provenance? The Droitwich brine salt springs are estimated to be approximately 200 million years old and are thought to be one of the purest in the world! This 100% natural product is sourced from the pumproom less than 3 miles away from the Saltworks on our farm where the brine is gently crystallised using renewable energy, before being dried, harvested by hand and packaged on-site.

Today we collaborate with many like-minded farmers and local food producers who serve their customers and communities as sustainably as possible. We are stocked in many farm shops, restaurants and kitchens across the UK and sell directly from our website. At our first Ludlow Food Festival we met Michelin-starred chef Brad Carter from Carters of Moseley (Birmingham). He was so blown away by the purity and flavour of our salt that he became our Salt Ambassador, singing our praises, nominating Droitwich Salt to be added to the prestigious Ark of Taste as well stocking our salt in his own shop. He also created a number of gourmet flavoured salts which subsequently won awards, based on the already award-winning original pure natural Droitwich Salt. Brad very kindly provided us with the recipe we have shared in this book, which champions autumnal, slow food ingredients and is of course, seasoned with our Droitwich Salt.

BRAD CARTER'S PHEASANT DUMPLINGS WITH SQUASH BROTH AND PUMPKIN OIL

Seasonal ingredients shine in this delicious slow food autumnal dish by our Salt Ambassador, Michelin-starred chef Brad Carter.

For the dumplings

450g minced pheasant meat

50g oats

8g Droitwich Salt

8g white pepper

6 sprigs of thyme, leaves picked and chopped

4 sage leaves, chopped

1 free-range egg

Dash of white wine

1 pack of wonton pastry squares

1 tbsp cornflour, mixed with cold water to make a thin paste

For the broth

250g butter

2 kabocha or acorn squash, peeled and chopped into small cubes

1 large banana shallot, chopped

1 clove of garlic, chopped

Pinch of cayenne pepper

500ml water or vegetable stock

1 orange, zested and juiced

To serve

100g pumpkin seeds

100ml virgin pumpkin seed oil

1 orange

For the dumplings

Mix all the ingredients except the pastry and cornflour together. Roll the mixture into balls weighing approximately 35g each.

Lay one sheet of wonton pastry on a board and brush with the cornflour mixture. Place a pheasant ball on top and lay another pastry sheet over that. Press down to seal and stick. Cut around the pheasant mixture using a pastry cutter to neaten the dumpling. Continue this process until you have used all the pheasant balls. Rest the dumplings in the fridge for at least an hour.

For the broth

Heat half the butter in a large saucepan. Very gently fry the pumpkin, shallot and garlic until softened, but not coloured (this will take around 20 to 30 minutes). Add the cayenne pepper, stock or water, remaining butter and a little salt, then cook for around 10 minutes over a medium heat until tender. Add the orange zest and juice. Pour the mixture into a blender, blitz and pass through a fine sieve. Season the broth with salt and pepper to taste.

Steam the dumplings in a steamer or in a colander over a pan of boiling water for around 7–8 minutes, or until the filling is cooked through and reads 65°c on a cooking thermometer.

To serve

While the dumplings cook, toast the pumpkin seeds in a dry pan until fragrant. Divide the steamed dumplings between deep, wide bowls and spoon over the pumpkin broth. Garnish with the toasted seeds and pumpkin seed oil. Grate some fresh orange zest over the top and serve immediately.

PREPARATION TIME: 30-40 MINUTES | COOKING TIME: 30 MINUTES | SERVES 4-6

E. OLDROYD & SONS

BY JANET OLDROYD HULME

"I am as determined as ever, together with my sons, to ensure the future of Yorkshire forced rhubarb and the industry producing it by keeping costs affordable and raising its profile."

In 1930 my great-grandfather left farming in Cambridgeshire to begin the family's association with forced rhubarb in Wakefield. My father Ken was determined to hold the declining rhubarb growers together by forming a cooperative, so in 1967 the Yorkshire Rhubarb Growers was established at our Carlton Farm. In recognition of his service to the industry over the following years, Ken was awarded the Northern Horticultural Society's highest accolade, The Harlow Carr Medal, in 1995 and became known by the media as the Rhubarb King!

Today our family business, E. Oldroyd & Sons Ltd, has five generations of experience in forced rhubarb production and is run by myself and my sons, Lindsay and James. I joined the business in 1980 and was shocked to see how much this world-renowned industry had declined. We had to open the bottle neck by increasing demand, which meant making the public more aware of the health benefits English fruit and veg can give us. In 1996 I was approached by Wakefield Council who wanted to use the local forced rhubarb industry in their regeneration program to promote local tourism. I wasn't sure it would work but we put talks and tours together which eventually developed into a festival that still takes place every February.

The awards and nominations followed thick and fast, from Rick Stein Food Hero to Young British Grower of the Year, and in 2010 Yorkshire forced rhubarb was finally given Protected Designation of Origin status. Our company is currently committed to an expansion program in all sectors of production, from crop rotation to constructing new forcing sheds heated by a sustainable energy production system. We also have a hedge and native tree planting scheme underway, not only for crop protection but to prevent soil erosion and as a wildlife habitat and food source, and have installed a bore hole to supply irrigation for the strawberry plantations.

I am as determined as ever, together with my sons, to ensure the future of Yorkshire forced rhubarb and the industry producing it by keeping costs affordable and raising its profile. We may not have been among the first families to force rhubarb in 1877 but we are one of the remaining 11 growers in the historic rhubarb triangle, where there were initially over 200. Our hard work aims to prevent all of us from being the very last of these skilled farmers.

JANET'S RHUBARB PANNA COTTA

You will require six glass dishes for this recipe, which makes the pink and cream colours look delightful. I prefer to leave the panna cotta in the dishes, preventing any mishaps when serving. If you do want to turn them out, don't forget to grease the dishes beforehand.

For the panna cotta

6 sheets of leaf gelatine

600ml (1 pint) single cream

300ml (10fl oz) double cream

85g (3oz) caster sugar

1 tbsp vanilla extract

For the rhubarb topping

2 sheets of leaf gelatine

800g forced rhubarb

85ml (3fl oz) pure orange juice

85g (3oz) caster sugar

Mint sprigs or edible flowers, to garnish

For the panna cotta

Soak the gelatine leaves in a small bowl of cold water for about 10 minutes until soft. Meanwhile, combine the creams and sugar for the panna cotta in a saucepan over a medium heat. Bring to the boil, stirring gently until the sugar has dissolved. Remove from the heat just as it starts to boil.

Remove the gelatine leaves from the water, squeezing gently to remove excess liquid, then add them to the warm cream and stir until completely dissolved. Stir in the vanilla extract, then pour the mixture into a large jug (this makes it easier to fill the dishes). Pour the panna cotta mixture carefully into your 6 glass dishes, leaving enough room for the rhubarb topping.

Allow to cool for around 30 minutes before covering with cling film and chilling the dishes in the fridge overnight. The panna cotta should be set and firm to the touch.

For the rhubarb topping

Soak the gelatine leaves in a small bowl of cold water for about 10 minutes until soft. Meanwhile, wipe the rhubarb with damp kitchen roll to clean it and then cut into small chunks. If you're making this in summer, use 400g of outdoor rhubarb and 400g of hulled and sliced British strawberries for great colour and a lovely tangy flavour.

In a pan, combine the orange juice (for a special occasion, try replacing this with sparkling wine) with the sugar and then add the rhubarb chunks. Simmer gently until the sugar has dissolved and the rhubarb is cooked, then squeeze out the soaked gelatine leaves and stir them into the pan until completely dissolved. Transfer the rhubarb mixture to a glass bowl and cover with cling film.

Once the panna cotta has set firm, carefully spoon over the cooled rhubarb mixture and smooth out. Finish with sprig of fresh mint or edible flower placed on top before serving.

PREPARATION TIME: 30 MINUTES, PLUS CHILLING OVERNIGHT | COOKING TIME: 30 MINUTES | SERVES 6

ECO EWE

BY OLIVIA SHAVE

"We are so proud to produce British lamb and share our farming journey, enthusing people to really connect with their food and to understand the effort that goes into it."

I am a Norfolk Shepherdess, based in the Brecks, where my ancient heritage breed of Norfolk Horns graze to conserve and restore the natural beauty and diversity of the sandy soils. The area is renowned for its unique geography and the way we farm here aims to restore the delicate ecology of our free-draining soil, while producing Great Taste award-winning lamb.

As a first-generation farmer, I run the business alongside my husband and two daughters. We started seven years ago after we suffered the very sad loss of my father-in-law, John. He had worked the land for over 45 years and passed his passion for the countryside onto my husband, Justin, and subsequently onto his grand-daughters, Jenna and Abi. He played an integral part in all our lives, and it seemed only fitting to continue his legacy, not only uniting us in grief but giving us all a purpose. 2021 brought one of our proudest achievements to date, when we became finalists in the prestigious Clarissa Dickson Wright category of the Countryside Alliance Awards, which recognise rural businesses that go the extra mile and were a huge honour for us.

Aside from the Norfolk Horns, we also have a starter flock of Charollais which we bought as a 21st birthday present for Abi so she can establish herself as a young female farmer. In addition, our North England mules provide us with the dual benefits of wool and meat, establishing a fully sustainable business. We are so proud to produce British lamb and share our farming journey, enthusing people to really connect with their food and to understand the effort that goes into it. This includes the high welfare standards we strive to achieve, all while conserving a heritage breed, giving back to our environment through regenerative farm practices, and enabling our daughters to enter an agriculturally based business.

It's vitally important to engage with the younger generation to share the realities of how British farmers are committed to producing healthy food while embracing the challenges of climate change, enabling them to make informed choices when it comes to eating balanced diets and buying local. I reach out to schools, pubs, restaurants and more through my roles as a Community Supporter for Love British Food and as a 'Lambassador' for AHDB which generally receives a great response. We also achieved a Great Taste award in 2020 and are hoping we can continue to put our lamb on lots of plates by advocating for its versatility and health benefits when farmed with pride.

NORFOLK LAMB MOUSSAKA

An ode to our award-winning rare breed Norfolk Horn lamb, encompassing our heritage and provenance with a twist. We've swapped the traditional white potatoes for sweet ones, which complements the natural notes of pasture and foraging which are evident in this beautiful meat.

750g lamb mince

1 onion, finely chopped

2 cloves of garlic, crushed

3 heaped tsp dried oregano

2 tsp ground cinnamon

2 bay leaves

Pinch of salt

Freshly ground black pepper

½ tbsp light brown soft sugar

2 tbsp tomato purée

200ml red wine

400g tinned chopped tomatoes

6 tbsp rapeseed oil

3 medium aubergines, thinly sliced

550g sweet potatoes, peeled and thinly sliced

For the bechamel sauce

40g unsalted butter

40g plain flour

400ml whole milk

30g parmesan, finely grated

½ nutmeg, finely grated

1 large free-range egg, beaten

Place the lamb, onion, crushed garlic, oregano, cinnamon and bay leaves into a heavy-based frying pan and cook for 8-10 minutes on a medium heat. Break up the mince using a wooden spoon.

Once the lamb has browned, drain off any excess fat. Continue to cook the mince mixture as you stir in a good pinch of salt and pepper with the sugar, tomato purée, red wine and tinned tomatoes. Bring to a gentle simmer and then leave to cook for a further 30 minutes, stirring occasionally until the lamb has tenderised.

Meanwhile, heat a frying pan over a high heat. Drizzle the oil over the sliced aubergine and fry for 4-5 minutes on both sides until golden brown. Set aside on kitchen paper to soak up any excess oil.

Preheat the oven to 200°c/180°c fan/Gas Mark 6 and bring a large pan of lightly salted water to the boil. Add the sweet potato slices to the pan and cook for 6 minutes, then drain in a colander under cold running water before placing on kitchen paper to drain.

For the bechamel sauce

Melt the butter in a small saucepan, gradually whisk in the flour and cook over a medium heat for 1 minute. Remove from the heat, slowly adding the milk and ensuring you continue to whisk until the sauce is smooth. Return to the heat and gently simmer for 3 minutes while stirring in the parmesan, grated nutmeg, and seasoning to taste. Let the sauce cool to room temperature before whisking in the beaten egg.

Spoon a third of the lamb mixture into a large ovenproof dish and spread out evenly, followed by a third each of the aubergine and potato slices. Repeat twice more to create distinct layers, then finish by pouring the bechamel sauce over the top and smoothing it out so you have an even covering. Sprinkle the moussaka with extra grated parmesan if you like, then place in the preheated oven for 35-45 minutes or until you have a nicely golden topping. Serve with a delicious herby green garden salad.

ELSTON FARM

· ·

BY ANDY GRAY

"I have an ingrained, historical love of farming, the outdoors, and the landscape of Devon. That doesn't mean I have to be conventional."

Farmers nurture things: crops or livestock, we enjoy looking after them and giving them the best chance to thrive. At Elston Farm we believe nurturing our soil is part of that process and helps rear healthy animals. Our growing interest in using natural processes is unendingly exciting and provides us with a great environment which we're filling with wildlife, and in which we also thrive.

Our ethos is sell it, then grow it. I have never grown anything I hadn't already had a customer for. I also find selling exciting; knowing I have a keen buyer for my produce completes the circle. We diversified into cider in 1666 so have always sold directly to the public. Our butchery business (M C Kelly Ltd) supplies restaurants but is also selling Farm Wilder meat boxes, which are available direct to the consumer.

I have an ingrained, historical love of farming, the outdoors, and the landscape of Devon. That doesn't mean I have to be conventional. The world changes, consumers' expectations change, science changes, and things often cycle back to where we started. The regenerative practices we are developing now are just our grandparents' practices but backed by better science and a societal need. They are also a marketing story; regenerative farming is what the public wants and will want increasingly as the benefits of these practices become ever more apparent: more nature, cleaner water, more delicious food, lower production costs, less flooding, to name just a few.

I came to Elston Farm in 1990 as an employee in the meat business. Primogeniture (meaning the first born inherits the family farm in this case) meant I had to take the long route to farming, build up an existing business and finally collude with the bank to buy my own farm. Elston Farm has exceptional soils tilting mainly to the south; it can grow almost anything. Years of arable have worn the soils out though, so we are adding livestock and developing a biodiversity-building, carbon capturing, pasture-based rotation by shifting the emphasis back to natural processes and reducing the use of chemicals.

Devon is one of the greatest meat producing counties in Europe; we have the climate, the soils and the farmers. We are exhorted to eat less meat to save the planet by the less scientifically literate; and to eat less but better, by those with a clearer grasp. As regenerative farmers we know this current zeitgeist still misses the point, that mixed farming and pasture-based farming locks up carbon, while cropping generally releases it. We also produce the most delicious pasture-fed meats.

MEDITERRANEAN VEG ROASTED IN BEEF DRIPPING WITH CHORIZO, BASIL AND FETA

This recipe is based on my respect for and connection with the livestock we nurture, raise, slaughter and butcher. Meat should be treasured, respected, and fully utilised: nose to tail cooking. Adding beef dripping to any dish will add an extra layer of delicious flavour.

For the dripping

Beef fat

Traditional kidney fat

For the meal

3-4 potatoes

1 butternut squash

1 aubergine

2 courgettes

2 mixed peppers (such as orange and red)

1 red onion

4 cloves of garlic

Plain flour, to dust

3 sprigs of thyme

200g cherry tomatoes

1 chorizo sausage

Handful of basil leaves

1 lemon, zested

50g feta, crumbled

Remove any gristle or sinew from the beef fat and traditional kidney fat. Place all the prepared fat into a heavy-bottomed casserole dish and cook in a preheated oven at 160°c for 1-2 hours, allowing the fat to render (melt) completely. Remove all the impurities and crispy bits, then decant the rendered fat into glass jars and store in the fridge.

When your dripping is ready, peel and dice the potatoes and then boil or steam until part cooked. Meanwhile, heat the oven to 180°c and prepare the other vegetables. Peel the squash, top and tail the aubergine and courgettes, deseed the peppers and then cut everything into chunks. Peel the onion and cut into wedges. Smash the garlic cloves, leaving the skins on.

Add a heaped tablespoon of dripping to a roasting tin and place in the oven to melt. Lightly dust your par-cooked potatoes with flour, then add them to the preheated roasting tin along with your prepared vegetables, onion and garlic. Make sure it's all evenly coated in the flavoursome dripping.

Place the roasting tin back into the oven and let the vegetables roast for 30 minutes. Give them a stir, then add the thyme, cherry tomatoes, and chunks of chorizo. Roast for a further 15 minutes.

To serve

Remove the thyme from the roasting tin, squeeze the softened garlic out of the skins to mix with the vegetables and chorizo, then scatter over the basil, lemon zest and crumbled feta to finish.

PREPARATION TIME: 30 MINUTES | COOKING TIME: 1-2 HOURS RENDERING, 45 MINUTES ROASTING | SERVES 4-6

EVG EUROPE

BY FRANCESCA BILLE

"Farming British produce is so important to us and all we do ensures that we get the best quality and healthiest vegetables to our customers."

EVG Europe began as a family business in 1976 founded by brothers Peter and Paul, and is now run by their sons, Andrew and Marco. Today we specialise in premium tomatoes, grown in our own glasshouses, as well as salad onions and asparagus, all grown in the Vale of Evesham.

Farming British produce is so important to us and all we do ensures that we get the best quality and healthiest vegetables to our customers. This would not be possible without the hard work of our farming, production, and sales teams. Our colleagues are the strength of EVG, with their knowledge and expertise guaranteeing we maximise our British production.

Sustainability is at the heart of our business, as we aim to become net zero in carbon emissions by 2040. Our latest glasshouse, called La Serra Ltd, is one of the most technologically advanced in Europe. We use state of the art lighting and heating technologies that enable us to grow British tomatoes all year round.

We have a solar farm and two anaerobic digestion plants which convert food waste and forage crops into renewable gas to grid, electric, food-grade CO_2 and digestate. The gas and electric are used to heat and light La Serra glasshouse and any we haven't used is injected into the National Grid to be used in your homes! Nothing is wasted and we spread the digestate back onto our fields, to aid the growth of the next crops and ensure our soil is as healthy as possible.

An important date in our calendar is the British Tomato Fortnight which runs for two weeks from late May to early June. The fortnight is a celebration of British Tomatoes and the different varieties all our nation's growers produce. So, next time you head to the supermarket or your local farm shop, make sure your tomatoes are British!

FRESH TOMATO, PANCETTA AND CHILLI PENNE

EVG Europe's historic roots lie in Italy, so it's no surprise that we love pasta. This quick pasta dish uses our own fresh cherry tomatoes: crisp and bursting with flavour! It's so simple yet absolutely delicious.

2 tbsp olive oil

2 cloves of garlic, minced

200g pancetta cubes

400g cherry tomatoes on the vine, halved

2 tsp chilli flakes

400g fresh penne pasta (other short pastas work well too)

½ pack of fresh basil leaves

Salt, to taste

Heat the olive oil and minced garlic in a large, non-stick pan over a medium heat. When the garlic begins to brown, add the pancetta and fry for 5 minutes.

Next, add the cherry tomatoes and chilli flakes, and simmer for 8-10 minutes. Meanwhile, fill a large pan three-quarters full of cold water and bring to the boil.

Once the water is boiling, add the pasta and salt to taste. Cook until al dente, then transfer a ladle of pasta water to the tomato sauce before draining the pasta.

Add the drained pasta to the tomato sauce and stir until evenly coated. Fold though the fresh basil leaves and serve straightaway.

PREPARATION TIME: 15 MINUTES | COOKING TIME: 20 MINUTES | SERVES 4

EWE MATTER (WOODBURY RYELANDS)

BY CLARE PRICE

"We have also seen a huge change in people's food buying habits. We wanted to develop the production and supply of our grass-fed native sheep, because provenance and food miles have become so important in those consumer choices."

Being a farmer's daughter and an active member of Young Farmers, my passion for agriculture developed very quickly. From a young age my main interest was in cows and sheep; from the age of six I was helping my dad feed calves and lambs. This soon developed into a passion for the British Simmental cattle breed, and I have now been a member of the British Simmental Cattle Society for 30 years. We have won many rosettes at national and local shows in that time. I won the Old Student Award at Warwickshire College and continuously support new entrants into the industry as a mentor for the Lord Plumb Foundation.

Having met my husband Richard at college, my passion for farming continued alongside my involvement with his farm management roles. We have always managed farming companies and estates for private owners but have continued to breed our own pedigree herd of Simmentals and a small flock of pedigree Ryeland sheep, which belong to our seven-year-old son. Mathew is so passionate about his sheep and has learnt commitment and routine through ensuring that they are healthy on a daily basis. He won a second-place rosette at Great Gransden show in the 2021 Young Handlers' class, which he richly deserved having spent many hours halter training his lambs.

Richard started his farm management career in 2001 at the Warwickshire College farm and then progressed to director of farming on the Lowther Estate, Cumbria. Richard won the Farmers Weekly Farm Manager of the Year in 2013 and Northern Farmer of the Year in 2014. In 2019, we moved to the Tetworth Estate in Bedfordshire as estate manager. Throughout both our careers, livestock and farming have been our passion and we are fortunate to have been able to work within this wonderful industry.

Agriculture is ever-changing with considerable challenges ahead. Environmental practices are crucial for sustainability, but so is producing a high-quality traceable product. Production has to work hand in hand with environmental good practice and is constantly changing as we enhance carbon capture, reduce chemical use and encourage mixed farming practices. We have also seen a huge change in people's food buying habits. We wanted to develop the production and supply of our grass-fed native sheep, because provenance and food miles have become so important in those consumer choices. We've had a very positive response from people who get to know the story and see the passion behind what we are producing at Woodbury Ryelands.

SMOKED LEG OF LAMB

··

This recipe involves smoking a slow-grown leg of lamb on the barbecue, after which the meat is seared on the hot embers of the fire to give it that authentic barbecued look and taste.

Big K charcoal

Cherry wood (for flavour)

1 British leg of lamb

Harissa La'mmmmm'b Rub and Seasoning

First, light your charcoal in the barbecue. I use a Big Green Egg with a barbecue starter and Big K charcoal; good quality charcoal does make all the difference. When the charcoal in the starter is glowing, pour it into your barbecue and add more charcoal. If you have a temperature gauge, you are looking for it to reach around 120-140°c.

Depending on the flavour you are trying to achieve, place the lumps of wood around the edge of the coals, but not directly on top as it will burn away too quickly. In this recipe I like to use cherry wood for the sweet, mild and fruity flavour it gives the smoke.

If you have a heat deflector plate, make sure this is put back into the barbecue for indirect smoking. If you don't have one, push the coals to one side of the barbecue.

Prepare your leg of lamb by covering the whole thing with the harissa rub. This will form an outer crust, especially when seared. Now decide how you want your meat to be cooked and use a meat thermometer to achieve this. Place the thermometer into the thickest part of the leg. Mine is linked to an app on my phone which tells me when the meat is done to my specific requirements, but as a general guide here are the temperatures you're looking for:

Rare = 48-54°c | Medium-Rare = 55-59°c
Medium = 60-66°c | Well-Done = 67-74°c

Place the leg of lamb directly onto the grill and close the lid of the barbecue. Don't be tempted to keep peeking at it. Be patient and wait for the smoking process to happen. After 3-4 hours, the smoking process should be complete, depending on how you like your lamb cooked (give it less time for rare, more for well-done – the exact times will depend on the size).

Now ramp up the heat ready for searing the lamb. This is a quick blast on the coals to give it a barbecued look. Blow the ash off the coals and drop the lamb onto the red-hot embers to sear on each side. Make sure you use some barbecue gloves so you can turn the lamb without getting burnt.

Let the meat rest before slicing and serving. We love this with the Oak Smoked Garlic Dauphinoise from the first edition of For The Love of the Land!

PREPARATION TIME: 20 MINUTES | COOKING TIME: 3-4 HOURS (DEPENDING ON SIZE) | SERVES 4 (DEPENDING ON SIZE)

THE FARMER'S SON

BY PETE MITCHELL

"I'm the ninth generation of our family to continue this proud tradition of delivering exceptional quality food, sustainably and ethically produced, with outstanding flavour."

My earliest memories as a boy were on our farm, running across pigsty roofs, playing in the bales, riding in the tractors. I always knew I would be involved in food and farming and I'm so proud of what we have created at The Farmer's Son. After returning to our family farm in my 30s, I wanted to build something that championed British farming and producers.

My family's farming roots in Scotland date back to the 1700s where for nearly 300 years we've reared livestock and produced crops while caring for the environment. We still farm and produce award-winning artisan produce which is the foundation of The Farmer's Son. I'm the ninth generation of our family to continue this proud tradition of delivering exceptional quality food, sustainably and ethically produced, with outstanding flavour.

At The Farmer's Son we believe there are few things in life more important than the food you eat. Our award-winning Scottish black pudding, haggis and white pudding products include home-grown, high welfare pork from our family farm and the finest locally sourced ingredients such as Scottish oatmeal from surrounding farms. These products are expertly handcrafted in small batches to a hundred-year-old family recipe with all natural Scottish ingredients and we pride ourselves on the quality, traceability, heritage and provenance of everything we create here in the beautiful Fife countryside.

Our small family farm of 247 acres is where we rear pigs and cattle as well as growing crops, including wheat and barley which is used for animal food and bedding. We have three wind turbines to create renewable energy and use the farmyard manure as a natural fertiliser to spread on the fields. We believe it's important to care for the planet for the next generation, so we reduce our food and supplier miles wherever possible.

Our customer base has grown over the years to now include many of the finest farm shops and food halls the country has to offer. We are so proud to have supplied many of the country's best chefs and won numerous awards. 2021 was one of our best years yet, with a Great Taste Gold Award, a Great British Food Award, and winning the Scottish Retail Food & Drink Awards. For us, it's a small acknowledgement of all the hard work we put in, but as they say, the proof really is in the pudding. We hope you love our products too.

HAGGIS TART WITH ZINGY SLAW

A delicious lunch, or perfect for summer entertaining, the open tart is given a Scottish twist with haggis. The slaw provides the perfect crunch to go with it. When busy on the farm, we're always looking for quick yet tasty meals and this is one of our favourites.

For the tart

1 pack of ready-rolled puff pastry

1 large red onion

2 cloves of garlic

2 peppers (1 red, 1 yellow)

8 mushrooms

Olive oil

220g haggis

1 goat's cheese log

1 egg yolk, beaten

Handful of grated cheddar cheese

Salt and pepper

For the slaw

¼ of a red cabbage

¼ of a white cabbage

1 carrot

1 apple

½ lime

Small bunch of fresh coriander

100g yoghurt

For the tart

Preheat the oven to 220°c. Unroll the puff pastry sheet without removing the baking paper it was wrapped in and lay it on a baking tray. Cut the pastry into 4 equal pieces, then lightly score a line around the edge of each piece to create a 1cm border.

Now prepare the vegetables by finely dicing the onion, garlic, peppers and mushrooms. Add a little olive oil to a frying pan and place over a medium heat. Gently sweat the onions for 3 minutes, then toss in the garlic. Add the peppers, giving them a few minutes to soften before adding the mushrooms for a final 2 minutes. Meanwhile, roughly chop up the haggis and slice the goat's cheese into rounds. Put them to one side.

Brush the pastry with the beaten egg yolk, then spoon the cooked vegetables evenly onto the pieces. Scatter over the haggis and lay the slices of goat's cheese on top, again dividing them evenly between the tarts. Sprinkle each one with a little grated cheese and season well. Bake the tarts in the preheated oven for 20 minutes, or until the pastry is golden and the cheese has melted.

For the slaw

While the tarts are baking, make your slaw. Finely shred the cabbage, grate the carrot and apple, juice the lime and finely chop the coriander. Combine all the ingredients in a bowl and season well.

Serve the tarts with the crunchy fresh slaw for the perfect summer lunch. If you want to try any variations on this recipe, black pudding makes a delicious substitute for the haggis. For vegetarians, brie also goes fabulously with courgette. These tarts are incredibly versatile, so enjoy experimenting.

PREPARATION TIME: 20 MINUTES | COOKING TIME: 20 MINUTES | SERVES 4

FARRINGTON'S MELLOW YELLOW

BY DUNCAN FARRINGTON

"I became incredibly passionate about the fantastic culinary and health properties of those little black seeds... With a high smoke point of 230°c plus a delicious nutty and buttery flavour, I knew that British cold pressed rapeseed oil could be a huge success."

I was born and brought up in the Northamptonshire village of Hargrave on a medium-size, arable family farm as a fourth-generation farmer. When I returned to the farm after university, I quickly realised that growing crops and driving tractors would not be enough to sustain my family for further generations, so I returned to my university research on cold pressed rapeseed oil.

I became incredibly passionate about the fantastic culinary and health properties of those little black seeds. My research showed that cold pressed rapeseed oil had half the saturated fat of olive oil and ten times the Omega 3, as well as naturally occurring vitamin E and plant sterols, making it a brilliantly healthy choice. With a high smoke point of 230°c, ideal for all types of roasting, frying, baking and dressing, plus a delicious nutty and buttery flavour, I knew that British cold pressed rapeseed oil could be a huge success.

In 2005, I launched the UK's first 'seed-to-bottle' cold pressed rapeseed oil, called Farrington's Mellow Yellow. I converted a small corner of one of our grain barns and installed a single press. Farrington's Mellow Yellow was a success, and it wasn't long before national supermarkets became interested in this fantastic British product and the business really took off. Along the way, my wife Eli, with her superior taste buds, has expanded the range to include salad dressings and infused oils from recipes created in our farmhouse kitchen. Now we're stocked in multiple national retailers, used in Michelin-starred restaurants and that single press in the corner of a barn has expanded to 12 presses, with more on the way, and a full professional food production facility!

Sustainability and the environment have always been at the heart of our business and something I am personally very passionate about, so all the rapeseed grown for Farrington's Mellow Yellow is grown to LEAF (Linking Environment And Farming) Marque standards. I am committed to sustainable farming practises, from the wildlife habitats around field edges, to the health of the soils in my fields, to solar panels on barn roofs powering our oil presses. In 2020 I was incredibly proud when Farrington Oils became the world's first food business to be certified as both carbon and plastic neutral and, in 2021, we were honoured to receive a Queen's Award for Enterprise for Sustainable Development for our industry-leading commitment to the environment.

BEETROOT AND CHOCOLATE CAKE

This is one of our favourite cake recipes made with Farrington's Mellow Yellow Rapeseed Oil and takes inspiration from the wartime tradition of using beetroot in cakes when cocoa was rationed. The combination of chocolate and beetroot creates an incredibly rich and indulgent cake that always goes down well!

200g plain cooked beetroot, well drained

30g cocoa powder

115g plain flour

1 ½ tsp baking powder

Pinch of salt

150g caster sugar

240ml Farrington's Mellow Yellow Rapeseed Oil

1 tsp vanilla extract

3 eggs, beaten

150g dark chocolate, chopped

Preheat your oven to 180°c or 160°c fan. Grate the cooked beetroot into a bowl and put to one side. Grease an 18cm (7 inch) round cake tin with a little Farrington's Mellow Yellow Rapeseed Oil and line with greaseproof paper.

Sift the cocoa powder, flour, baking powder and salt into a large mixing bowl and stir in the sugar. Add the grated beetroot, Farrington's Mellow Yellow Rapeseed Oil, vanilla extract, eggs and dark chocolate and mix well.

Pour your cake batter into the prepared tin and bake for 1 hour in the preheated oven, until a skewer comes out clean. It will be fairly moist and fudgy in the middle.

Allow the cake to cool for a few minutes in the tin once baked and then turn out onto a wire rack to fully cool. Enjoy with a cup of tea and good company.

F B PARRISH AND SON

JAMES AND NICK PARRISH

"A century of farming has given us a taste for good, wholesome food and we love experimenting with recipes that we can share with friends and family around the dining table. We hope that the recipes here instil in you the passion for food that we as British farmers share."

We are a family-run farm in the beautiful Bedfordshire countryside. Our farm has been managed by three generations of Parrish families, dating all the way back to 1927 when our grandfather, Frank Parrish, first bought the land for a dairy farm to supply the local villages with daily fresh milk.

For the last 30 years we've been utilising the rich, sandy soils of the Greensand Ridge to grow onions and shallots. Today, we farm over 150 acres of shallots that are neatly sown in lines, planted exactly 40mm apart and 20mm deep by automated tractors controlled by GPS technology. This combination of modern technology and traditional planning allows us to farm in the most effective ways, saving energy and reducing waste while growing quality products.

We are passionate about being at the forefront of sustainability and pride ourselves on being environmentally friendly, taking great care of the land that we farm on. Many of our fields are ringed by strips of uncultivated land, which are rich in wild flora and fauna to encourage biodiversity. We are also part of several biodiversity and wildlife programs and actively work to help monitor and grow the population of several local wildlife species here in Bedfordshire, including barn owls and pollinators such as bumblebees.

We have over 400kw of solar panels installed around the farm that produce the renewable energy we need to run our state-of-the-art storage facilities. This helps to ensure our produce is kept in the best condition for longer, in an environmentally friendly way.

Our produce is grown under the LEAF (Linking Environment and Farming) protocol, which is one of the leading environmental growing programmes in the UK. The LEAF approach is built around the whole-farm principles of Integrated Farm Management (IFM), which achieves a balance between the best modern technology and sound traditional methods, while enriching the environment.

A century of farming has given us a taste for good, wholesome food and we love experimenting with recipes that we can share with friends and family around the dining table. We're proud to be a part of this wonderful book and hope that the recipes here instil in you the passion for food that we as British farmers share.

SHALLOT AND POTATO CAKE

. . . .

Not your average potato cake! This hearty recipe makes the perfect side dish for a hot meal or salad and features two of our flagship products: banana shallots and King Edward potatoes. We personally love it alongside a roast dinner, and it can even be prepared ahead of time and reheated.

4 large potatoes

4 large echalion shallots (also called banana shallots)

1 tbsp olive oil

1 tbsp butter, plus 1 tsp for greasing

1 egg, beaten

2 tbsp sour cream

Salt and pepper

Nutmeg, to taste

Thyme leaves, to garnish

Bake the potatoes in their skins in a 200°c oven for an hour or more until fully cooked through. Allow to cool but leave the oven on.

Meanwhile, peel and slice the shallots and sauté over a low heat in the oil and butter for up to 40 minutes until soft and golden.

Halve the cooled potatoes and scoop the flesh out into a bowl. Break it up with a fork before adding the beaten egg, sour cream, seasoning and a grating of nutmeg to taste. Add the cooked shallots and gently mix.

Grease a cake tin with the teaspoon of butter and tip the potato mixture in, smoothing the surface with a spoon or spatula. Bake in the hot oven for 30 minutes or until golden.

Remove the tin from the oven and leave to cool slightly before running a knife around the edge and turning the potato cake out. Dress with a few thyme leaves to serve.

Recipe by www.ukshallot.com on behalf of Parrish Farms, using British-grown shallots and potatoes.

F B PARRISH AND SON

. . . .

PAGE 86

PREPARATION TIME: 20 MINUTES | COOKING TIME: 1 HOUR 30 MINUTES | SERVES 6 AS A SIDE

FOREST FUNGI

BY SCOTT MARSHALL

"With seven grow rooms on our two-acre Dawlish site producing over one tonne of mushrooms per week, we farm super intensively, producing a huge amount of food from a very small space."

I first fell in love with mushrooms while roaming the forests of Cambridgeshire and Devon. The idea of farming them came to me after discovering their medicinal benefits when I was diagnosed with cancer and underwent chemotherapy. I was hooked and left my well-paid career in retail management to pursue my new obsession. Having successfully trialled my first grows, I found our site (then derelict) and started to build my first grow room and our farm shop. My partner Becca soon quit her job to join me, and we opened our doors to the trade and public in July 2013, six months (and a lot of sweat and blood) later.

Two years later I met local and renowned chef, Andrew Milford-Dummet (aka Bruno). We became great friends and soon opened our café which showcases our and other local growers' products. Today, the mushroom farm is headed up by Dave Weymouth, Bruno's son-in-law, who continues to innovate. He is a huge part of the reason we are where we are, along with our loyal team of 14 people who have been integral in developing and growing this business.

With seven grow rooms on our two-acre Dawlish site producing over one tonne of mushrooms per week, we farm super intensively, producing a huge amount of food from a very small space. We use no chemicals in the process and grow our mushrooms on waste and by-products from the wood processing industry, using only sawdust, rye, spawn and water to let our climate control systems do the rest. We now grow nine different species throughout the year and have been lucky to work with some of the country's best chefs and retailers. Our home and heart remains in Devon though, and 90% of what we grow is sold within a 35 mile radius of our farm.

We have recently partnered with a new team of investors and are currently building a new state of the art farm just three miles from our current site. This will be capable of producing five tonnes of our gourmet mushrooms per week, enabling our rollout of a national supply using all of the same ethics and principles we have worked to over the years. We will use the recovered space on our current site to further develop our visitor experience, allowing our visitors to learn about and further understand the fantastic world of fungi in a hands-on way. This always has and always will be a family business, it's just a much bigger family now.

EGGS CHAMPIGNON

· ·

This recipe was developed by my friend and talented chef Andrew Milford-Dunnet, who sadly passed away a few years ago. It has become our signature dish at the Forest Fungi café and I'm proud to share it with you here.

7 large free-range eggs

1 tbsp lemon juice

1 tsp Dijon mustard

Salt and pepper

145g butter

250g Forest Fungi mixed mushrooms

2 English breakfast muffins

½ a lemon

25g fresh parsley, finely chopped

Smoked paprika or truffle dust, to finish

First, make the Hollandaise sauce. Separate 3 of the eggs and combine the yolks with the lemon juice, Dijon mustard and a pinch of salt and pepper in a blender. Blend on high power for 5 seconds. Melt 120g of the butter in a microwave for 1 minute. Gradually add the melted butter to the yolk mixture while continuing to blend until the sauce has emulsified to a smooth texture. Set aside.

Boil some water in a saucepan and leave to simmer ready for your poached eggs. Next, melt the remaining 25g of butter in a frying pan on a high heat. As the butter starts to brown, stir in the mushrooms so they are all coated. Leave on a high heat, stirring occasionally, for 7 minutes. You are aiming to brown the mushrooms as quickly as you can. Season with a good pinch of salt and pepper.

Meanwhile, halve and toast the breakfast muffins. Once the 7 minutes are up, carefully crack the remaining 4 eggs into the saucepan of simmering water to poach. This should take between 2 minutes and 2 minutes 30 seconds.

Place the toasted muffins cut side up on your serving plates. Take the mushrooms off the heat once fully cooked and quickly squeeze the fresh lemon juice over them. Stir in the parsley to finish them and taste to check the seasoning.

Evenly pile the mushrooms onto your halved muffins. Carefully place a poached egg on top of each stack. Spoon over your finished hollandaise sauce and garnish with smoked paprika or truffle dust and a little more parsley to serve.

PREPARATION TIME: 10 MINUTES | COOKING TIME: 15 MINUTES | SERVES 2

GLASS BROTHERS

. . . .

BY ROBERT BYRNE

"What matters to us is that we have nurtured our food from tree to customer. We are with it every step of the way until it leaves us."

Northern Ireland is a country of foodies who particularly like to eat food that's been farmed, harvested, processed and cooked or baked locally. Glass Brothers shares this obsession with food, and our love for the mighty Bramley is unrivalled! It's well-loved in the UK as the best apple for cooking and baking. Its unique flavour is due to the high level of malic acid and low level of sugar. This gives it a robust structure, flavour and acidic taste, suitable for almost all culinary recipes.

Glass Brothers have been a family business in County Armagh, Northern Ireland, since 1963. It began with our relatives, Wilson and Ivan Glass, growing and selling their own Bramley apples. The evolution of both UK and global manufacturing led the family to switch to fresh chilled production in 1998 and today we process the Bramley apple into a wide range of products from slices to purée. Despite the change in direction, the business has quite literally maintained its farming roots and is proud to remain family-run. We're also one of the few food producers who can say they've brought their food from tree to packaging!

We proudly manage all our own orchards, with a spray programme overseen by a fully qualified agronomist. This means the correct products are applied at the correct time to ensure maximum benefit in set, yield and quality. Harvest takes place annually from mid-September to the end of October. This is a manual process managed by us. Once picked, the fruit must be cooled and stored, ideally within 12 hours. To maintain these high standards, we recently upgraded our facilities by converting them all to ULO (Ultra Low Oxygen) storage which maintains the apples at 5% CO_2 and 1% O_2, preventing them from ripening without using chemicals or affecting the flavour and texture.

Our dedication to farming standards, quality control, storage and processing has been recognised with a BRC (British Retail Consortium) AA accreditation (its highest possible rating), as well as Red Tractor accreditation, and accreditation by the Global G.A.P. initiative. We may have pivoted into manufacturing, but what matters to us is that we have nurtured our food from tree to customer. We are with it every step of the way until it leaves us. That commitment to traceability, safety and food quality is what defines the best of British farming for us, and why we're so proud to work the land and help bring the best of it to people's plates.

APPLE, CHEESE AND THYME MUFFINS

We love this recipe which blends the trademark sharpness of the Bramley apple with savoury flavours for a comforting snack, delicious served warm or cold. It combines the Bramley with some other stars of British farming – cheddar cheese, creamy whole milk, fresh free-range eggs – and marries them with delicious and familiar flavours of Italy and Europe.

Oil or butter, for greasing

150g plain flour

75g fine polenta (cornmeal)

1 tsp baking powder

½ tsp sea salt

¼ tsp bicarbonate of soda (baking soda)

1 Bramley apple, peeled and chopped into small chunks

75g + 2 tbsp cheddar cheese, grated

2 tsp fresh thyme leaves

200ml whole milk

1 free-range egg, lightly beaten

1 tsp Dijon mustard

Preheat your oven to 190°c or 375°F. Lightly grease the cups of a muffin tray with cooking oil or butter. Sift the flour, polenta, baking powder, salt and bicarb of soda into a large bowl, then stir in the apple chunks, 75g of grated cheese and half the thyme (reserving the rest for decoration).

In a small bowl, lightly whisk the milk, egg and mustard together. Pour the milk mixture into the flour mixture and stir to combine.

Spoon the batter into the prepared muffin tray until the cups are three quarters full. Sprinkle the remaining 2 tablespoons of cheddar over the top.

Bake for 15 to 20 minutes in the preheated oven or until the muffins have risen and turned a light golden colour. Sprinkle the remaining thyme leaves onto the melted cheese.

Allow the muffins to cool in the tin for 5 minutes, then remove and cool completely on a wire rack.

These are perfect served with chilli jam to add a bit of spice!

PREPARATION TIME: 5-10 MINUTES | COOKING TIME: 15-20 MINUTES | MAKES 12

GOLDSLAND FARM

BY ABI READER MBE

"Farming as a job brings me pure joy, whether that's working with livestock, being out in the fresh air and the green grass, seeing the sunrise every morning, taking my dog to work and of course the quiet, peaceful surroundings rarely interrupted by anything other than birdsong."

I am a third generation farmer, farming along with my family. We run a traditional mixed farm of 200 dairy cows, 150 sheep, 100 beef cattle and some arable crops that we grow for home use as winter fodder and bedding. Farming as a job brings me pure joy, whether that's working with livestock, being out in the fresh air and the green grass, seeing the sunrise every morning, taking my dog to work and of course the quiet, peaceful surroundings rarely interrupted by anything other than birdsong and the odd moo or baa.

Our cows and sheep are descended from both sets of grandparents and my affinity with their bloodlines runs deep. Much of our farm is also still made up of old traditional stone buildings including our Grade II listed stone barn with its slit windows and impressive roof stretching high over my head. All this is coupled with modern investments we have made which offer more practical and state of the art facilities for today's livestock and the people who work here.

Looking into the future, my farm is committed to investing in more technology to improve the value and quality of the food we produce and also to reduce our carbon footprint. I really enjoy collaborating with others on different projects. We are a 'living lab' for trials in carbon sequestration, habitat creation, efficient grass growth and animal health.

At the core of anything we do is my determination to share our story with the wider world and to involve people in our journey, whether that's school children, youth groups, university students, nature groups and so many more. Once a year, usually the first Sunday in June, we throw our gates open for Open Farm Sunday; this is a national farming event inviting people to visit participating farms in their locality to meet the farmers and see what goes into producing their food.

Our farm has won various awards over the years for enhancing nature, carbon reduction and animal health and I was also honoured to receive an MBE in 2019 for Services to Farming. What I really want is for people to reach for British products when they go food shopping or eat out because they feel an affinity with farms, just like mine, who provide safe and traceable products they can trust.

WELSH LAMB AND CHEDDAR RISOTTO

I love this recipe; it's so easy to make and it all cooks in one pan which saves on washing up! Most of the ingredients are local to me: Welsh lamb, veg from my garden and of course being a dairy farmer, I finish the risotto with a little bit of butter and cheddar cheese which gives it a creamy consistency.

1 tsp oil

1 onion, chopped

1 leek, chopped

225g lean PGI Welsh lamb leg steaks, cut into small cubes

150g risotto (Arborio) rice

600ml stock

Black pepper

50g runner beans, thinly sliced

50g frozen peas

25g Welsh butter

50g mature Welsh cheddar cheese

Handful of rocket leaves or spinach

Heat the oil in a large saucepan or deep frying pan and cook the onion, leek and cubed lamb for 5 minutes until they start to brown. Add the risotto rice and stir thoroughly.

Pour the stock into the pan and bring to the boil, then stir well and season with black pepper. Simmer gently, stirring occasionally, for approximately 35 minutes or until the rice is cooked and all the liquid has been absorbed (you can add a little more stock to achieve your desired texture/consistency if needed).

During the last 5 minutes of the cooking, add the sliced runner beans and frozen peas, stir everything together and cook until the runner beans just start to soften.

Add the butter and mix well, then finish your risotto by grating over the cheese and serving it with a handful of rocket or spinach on top.

GOODWOOD

· ·

BY THE DUCHESS OF RICHMOND AND GORDON

"We believe that our relationship with the environment – both natural and built – shapes our physical and mental health."

The benefits of organic food and farming were impressed upon me at a relatively young age, as my mother, Bronwen Astor, had an organic kitchen garden in the 1970s, and my uncle, David Astor, founded the Organic Research Centre - the UK's leading research centre into organic farming - in 1981.

When I came to Goodwood, I was happy to discover that my mother-in-law, Susan, Duchess of Richmond and Gordon, shared my interest. She was an early member of the Soil Association, and together we spearheaded the conversion of Goodwood Home Farm to organic farming methods. Goodwood became the first 100% organically-fed dairy farm in the country and is now the largest lowland organic farm in Europe.

Paul Dovey, the farm manager, was one of the first batch of students to study Organic Agriculture at Derby college, a course set up by the Soil Association. He is passionate about animal welfare, as well as the importance of soil, which is at the centre of everything we do.

Organic principles enable us to produce the best-tasting beef, pork and lamb, all of which are reared on the farm. Our restaurant – Farmer, Butcher, Chef – is dedicated to showcasing our meat as well as achieving the best yield from our livestock. The butcher is directly involved in designing dishes according to the cuts available, which makes Goodwood as near to a completely closed system as possible.

We believe that our relationship with the environment – both natural and built – shapes our physical and mental health. Last year, we launched the Goodwood Gut Health Programme, a five-day restorative retreat designed to significantly improve your health and wellbeing. Developed by nutritionists Stephanie Moore and Elaine Williams, the aim is to improve digestive function and help you feel better in all aspects of your life. The programme makes the best use of the top-quality organic pasture-fed meat that we have on the farm and the beef recipe we have shared overleaf is one of my favourite dishes.

Photo © Jon Nicholson

ROAST RIBEYE OF BEEF WITH CULTURED CREAM AND FERMENTED LEEKS

· ·

This delicious and healthy dish is taken from the Goodwood Gut Health Programme. Fermented foods are rich in probiotic bacteria, which help to increase the health of your gut and enhance your immune system. Organic beef is rich in nutrients, including Omega 3 fatty acids.

For the fermented leeks

3 small leeks

1 clove of garlic

1 tsp coriander seeds

½ tbsp sea salt

Handful of fresh dill

For the cultured cashew cream

300g raw cashews

Filtered water

2 tbsp plain, unsweetened non-dairy or coconut yoghurt

½ tsp sea salt

For the steak and fresh vegetables

4 ribeye steaks

Flaky sea salt

Freshly ground black pepper

100g clarified butter

2 sprigs of fresh thyme

1 clove of garlic, bashed with skin left on

3 courgettes, thinly sliced

1 large bunch of asparagus

For the fermented leeks

These can be prepared up to 9 days in advance. Wash the leeks and thinly slice the white parts, discarding most of the green. Finely slice the garlic and mix it with the sliced leek, coriander seeds and salt. Finely chop the dill and add to the bowl, give everything a good massage, then transfer the mixture to a quart jar with an airlock and fill with water. Leave the jar at room temperature for 3-7 days away from sunlight, then transfer to the fridge for 2 more days.

For the cultured cashew cream

This can be prepared up to 3 days in advance. Soak the cashews overnight in filtered water. The next day, prepare a clean and dry glass (or other non-reactive) container. Drain the soaked cashews and blend until completely smooth to release oils, stopping to scrape down the sides if required. You can add filtered water a tablespoon at a time if you're having trouble blending them. Note: if the blender starts to warm up, take a break and wait for it to cool down as you can kill the cultures with heat!

Add the yoghurt and salt to the blender, pulse to combine, then transfer the mixture to the prepared container and cover. Let the cashew cream sit at room temperature for 24 hours, then taste and add more salt if required. Let it culture for another 12-24 hours if you would like a stronger tang.

For the steak and fresh vegetables

Cook these just before you want to serve the dish. Remove the steaks from the fridge half an hour before cooking, then season on both sides with salt and pepper. Heat the pan until it's nearly smoking, then add the steaks. Leave them for 5 minutes, then flip over and add half of the butter with the thyme and garlic. Tilt the pan and spoon the melted butter back over the steak. Cook for a further 5 minutes, depending on how you like your steak. For a 3cm thick ribeye, a rough guide is 8 minutes of total cooking time for medium-rare.

Meanwhile, heat the remaining butter in a frying pan and then cook the sliced courgettes for about 5 minutes, adding a little salt and pepper to taste. Boil the asparagus for 3 minutes in salted water.

To serve

Place the steak just off centre on the plate, next to a line of courgette with asparagus on top. Dot some of the cashew cream onto the asparagus, and a little more on the steak. Finish with a spoonful of the fermented leeks.

GOODWOOD

· ·

PAGE 102

THE GOURMET GOAT FARMER

BY LAURA CORBETT

"As a predominantly grazing herd, we aspire to make the goats even more central to our conservation efforts and take pride in growing as much of their diet as possible on the farm."

In 2017, we began a new chapter in our third-generation family business at East Farm in Wiltshire. I wanted to find a niche and explore my interest in goat farming, so today we are home to a herd of 250 Boer goats and employ a fabulous local team of six people who work with them, as well as selling our produce in the Farm Larder and at local markets.

Our efforts on the farm are centred around nurturing the needs of our breeding females so that we can depend on them to rear young as nature intended. We believe in the importance of family unity, and the security this gives the herd. Our goats browse in pastures and hedgerows, taking refuge inside their purpose-built spacious indoor housing when the unpredictable British weather turns. As a predominantly grazing herd, we aspire to make the goats even more central to our conservation efforts and take pride in growing as much of their diet as possible on the farm. In the height of summer, we make any surplus meadow grass into hay which is stored for winter feed.

I'm often asked 'why goats?' and my answer is always why not! The British have been used to eating lamb since the wool trade boom many centuries ago but as our nation got wealthier, the goat became a peasantry animal and left our culinary table. However, goat is said to be the most widely eaten red meat in the world, for good reason considering its nutritional benefits. Goat is reported to be higher in protein and iron than any other meat and the milk is highly digestible; team this with the animal's hardiness (goats can survive in extreme conditions unfit for cattle and sheep) and what's not to like?

During the pandemic, we teamed up with other struggling British goat farmers and started selling their dairy produce along with ours direct to the public. This offering now includes organic goat's milk, a range of fabulous goat's cheese from the southwest, soap and skin lotion, plus fibres from Angora goats such as mohair socks and skeins: all very proudly British and a one-stop shop for the best goat produce! This collaboration also allowed us to share our farming knowledge, which is proving invaluable for improving our animal husbandry and farm management. This in turn benefits nature and biodiversity on our farm, which is something we have been working towards for decades.

GOURMET GOAT FARMER The Larder

THE GOURMET GOAT FARMER

GOAT BIRYANI

· ·

This curry house favourite is meant to be shared so we encourage you to serve it from the dish at the table and let your guests enjoy the full aromas, accompanied by naan, raita and a simple tomato salad. It's a real crowd pleaser and well worth the effort.

200g natural yoghurt

100g fresh ginger, grated

8 cloves of garlic, crushed

2 fresh chillies, finely chopped (optional)

2 tbsp garam masala

3 tsp ground turmeric

2 tsp each ground coriander and cumin

1 tsp ground cinnamon

½ tsp chilli powder

1 lemon, juiced

Salt and pepper

2kg goat shoulder

3 tbsp rapeseed oil

2 onions, finely sliced

1 tbsp cumin seeds

8 cardamom pods

1 cinnamon stick

1 bay leaf

8 whole cloves

120g butter

400g basmati rice

200ml milk

Generous pinch of saffron strands

Handful of fresh coriander leaves, roughly chopped

Preparing the meat

Combine the yoghurt, ginger, garlic, fresh chillies (if using), ground spices (garam masala, 2 teaspoons of the turmeric, coriander, cumin, cinnamon and chilli powder) and lemon juice in a large bowl, then generously season with salt and pepper. Smother the goat shoulder in this mixture, then cover and leave to marinate in the fridge for a minimum of 6 hours or, better still, overnight.

An hour before cooking, remove the marinated goat from the fridge so it comes to room temperature. Preheat the oven to 230°c or 220°c fan. Place the shoulder in a large roasting tin and roast for 15 minutes in the preheated oven to brown in a few places. Turn the temperature down to 160°c or 150°c fan and add 250ml of boiling water to the roasting tin, then cover with a layer of baking parchment and a layer of foil, sealing tightly around the edges. Cook the shoulder in the oven for 3 hours 30 minutes.

Preparing the onions

Heat the rapeseed oil in a deep heavy-based pan over a high heat until it sizzles when a piece of onion is dropped in. Fry the finely sliced onions for 10 minutes until golden, then transfer to a plate lined with kitchen roll using a slotted spoon.

Preparing the rice

Fry the cumin seeds, cardamom pods, cinnamon stick, bay leaf and whole cloves in a saucepan with half the butter for 1 minute over a moderate heat. Add the remaining ground turmeric and the rice, then fry for another minute. Stir in 450ml of boiling water and a generous pinch of salt. Cook uncovered until the water has been absorbed (about 5 minutes).

Assembling and serving the dish

Heat the milk, then add the saffron and leave to infuse for at least 5 minutes. Meanwhile, grease an ovenproof casserole dish with butter. Layer the rice and onions in the dish with half the coriander leaves and dot with the remaining butter. Pour over the infused milk and saffron. Place the cooked goat meat on top and cover with baking parchment or foil before placing the lid on to retain as much steam as possible. Finish the biryani in the oven for 35-45 minutes at 170°c or 160°c fan. Remove the lid and scatter the remaining coriander leaves over the top to serve.

PREPARATION TIME: 6-24 HOURS MARINATING | COOKING TIME: 4 HOURS 30 MINUTES | SERVES 6

HEATHER HILLS FARM

BY MARK NOONAN

"Due to the unique nature of the honey, the climate, terrain and limited production season, it's a botanical labour of love but the reward is something incredibly rare and intensely aromatic."

Established from humble beginnings with a single hive in 1945, Heather Hills Farm is one of Scotland's leading and award-winning producers of artisan honeys and preserves, internationally recognised for their superior provenance, quality and flavour. With 1300 hives, the farm is run by brothers Mark and Bernard Noonan who were brought up in the glen of Strathardle, Perthshire, where the farm is based.

Our award-winning Scottish Heather Honey is our signatory honey and that of Scotland. Known as the Champagne of honeys, it's gathered from wild-flowering purple heather in the Scottish moors between July and September of each year. Due to the unique nature of the honey, the climate, terrain and limited production season, it's a botanical labour of love but the reward is something incredibly rare and intensely aromatic. Like a single malt whisky, its unique terroir dictates its outstanding autumnal palate, and – combined with its limited production season – makes it highly sought after.

We're dedicated to our cultural and natural heritage, the sustainability of the honeybee and its essential work in pollination. The Scottish weather combined with the decline of the honeybee is a constant challenge for us, but our small-scale production and well-spaced hives ensure our bees have enough forage to produce the finest honeys. These are collected and extracted using traditional methods – never heated over the normal temperature of the hive to ensure their inherent characters and natural benefits are not destroyed – before being bottled and labelled by hand in small batches.

Fruit culture has been part of our local heritage for over 100 years and in the spring of each year, we work with local Perthshire berry growers who depend on our 52 million worker bees to carry out the necessary pollination required for optimum crop yields and the perfect berry. In turn, our bees gather the nectar to produce our outstanding spring Scottish Blossom Honey while keeping our colonies strong for the heather season. It's a natural synergy and formative in our jam making. Each of our honeys and preserves are part of this very special relationship between our bees and the many foods they help to produce. This not only prevents the decline of the honeybee, but also supports the continued production of the best soft fruit in the world.

RASPBERRY CRANACHAN

This 'King of Scottish Desserts' marries the signature flavours of Scotland: heather honey, raspberries, oats and whisky. Traditionally made to celebrate the Scottish raspberry harvest in June, it is now part of our national identity and is a staple at Burns Supper on January 25th each year.

60g oatmeal

200g raspberries

1 tbsp icing sugar

600ml double cream

½ a vanilla pod

4 tbsp Scottish heather honey

3 tbsp malt whisky

Lightly toast the oatmeal in a dry frying pan over a medium heat until golden brown. Keep the oatmeal moving to prevent it from burning. Remove from the pan and allow to cool once done.

Place 100g of the raspberries in a food processor along with the icing sugar and blend to a smooth purée. Set aside.

In a large bowl, whisk the cream until it reaches soft peak consistency. Scrape out the contents of the vanilla pod and fold into the cream before folding in the heather honey and malt whisky.

Set aside 2 tablespoons of toasted oatmeal to garnish the cranachan, then add the rest of the oatmeal to the flavoured cream, folding in well.

To serve

Fold the raspberry purée into the cream mixture until you have a ripple effect. Spoon some of the remaining whole raspberries into the bottom of 6 glasses or ramekins, then add the cream mixture. Top with more raspberries and finish with a sprinkling of toasted oatmeal.

HOLKHAM

· ·

BY JAMES BEAMISH

"Our farmland is a rich tapestry of life: we create wide grass and wildflower margins; leave hedges to grow broad and tall to encourage richer biodiversity; champion cover-cropping, conservation and tree planting; and are working on restoring historic ponds. We believe farming and conservation go hand-in-hand."

Agriculture has always played a fundamental role at Holkham, and I am honoured to have the responsibility of managing our farming business today. Conservation and sustainability are at the heart of all our decision making, from the way we manage the farmland and Holkham National Nature Reserve to our attractions, parkland and gardens. In 2021 we launched WONDER, an action plan which sets out bold targets under the themes of championing low carbon living, stamping out waste and pioneering environmental gain.

Over 3000 hectares of estate land is managed by my team at the Holkham Farming Company. Our farmland is a rich tapestry of life: we create wide grass and wildflower margins; leave hedges to grow broad and tall to encourage richer biodiversity; champion cover-cropping, conservation and tree planting; and are working on restoring historic ponds. We believe farming and conservation go hand-in-hand, so much so that we now have a trial farm site on the estate which is entirely dedicated to pushing the boundaries of this relationship.

Arable farming, conservation and livestock can be seen living alongside each other across the entire estate. Belted Galloways graze on the Holkham National Nature Reserve (NNR) throughout the warmer months, and our flocks of sheep are integrated as a grazing tool around the park and farmland. The herd of cattle are hardy and adaptable and, together with our sheep and the deer from within the park, provide good quality meat to local butchers, Holkham's three cafés and The Victoria, our hotel and restaurant which sits on the edge of the NNR.

When it comes to cropping, we are fortunate to be in what is classed as the 'champagne' region of malting barley, and we now partner Adnams in Suffolk with a large proportion of the barley used to brew their award-winning ales. We also grow sugar beet, which is supplied to British Sugar, as well as wheat, oilseed rape, beans and maize. The latter is used in the anaerobic digestion plant we have onsite, which creates enough energy to power our local area and a soil improver that goes back onto our land. Alongside this, we also have a solar farm.

The collective knowledge and expertise between myself and my colleagues Jake Fiennes (conservation), Harry Wakefield (forestry) and Mark Fitzer (game keeping) makes us a formidable team and it is this rare mix, together with our vision and ambitions at Holkham, that allows us to forge ahead and lead the way in influencing positive change.

FAGGOTS, POMME PURÉE AND HORSERADISH JUS

· ·

Michael Chamberlain, head chef of The Victoria at Holkham, produced this hearty dish to satisfy Lord Leicester's love of traditional food while minimising waste. His faggots are made using leftover beef from our Belted Galloway herd and offal from the estate's lambs, creating something delicious from what might otherwise be thrown away.

For the faggots

50g salted butter

I small onion, finely diced

2 cloves of garlic, grated

10g sage, finely chopped

10g picked thyme

500g minced beef

100g lamb's heart, finely diced

100g lamb's liver, finely diced

100g lamb's kidney, finely diced

200g smoked bacon, finely diced

5g each salt and pepper

2 eggs

100g breadcrumbs (more if the mix is wetter)

Caul fat, to wrap

I litre vegetable stock

For the pomme purée

800g Maris Piper potatoes

200ml milk

75g salted butter

For the horseradish jus

500ml veal stock (or beef stock if you don't have veal)

40g horseradish sauce

25g salted butter

For the faggots

Heat the butter in a heavy-based pan. Sweat off the onion, garlic and herbs and set to one side.

In a bowl, combine the mince, offal, bacon, onion mix, salt, pepper and egg. Mix well, then add enough breadcrumbs to make an easy-to-shape ball that is not too sticky and does not break up.

Roll the mixture into 125g balls and wrap each one in the caul fat. Place the balls into a deep casserole dish and add enough vegetable stock to come halfway up the balls. Drizzle with oil and cover, then bake at 180°c for 2 hours 45 minutes.

For the pomme purée

While the faggots are baking, boil the potatoes until soft and allow to drain well. Put the milk and butter in the pan and heat until reduced by one third. Return the potatoes to the pan, mash until smooth and season to taste.

For the horseradish jus

Boil the veal or beef stock until it has reduced by half. Once reduced, add the horseradish sauce.

Whisk in the butter to thicken the jus as you are ready to serve.

To serve

Place a large serving spoonful of mash in the centre of the plate, place the faggots on top and nappe (coat) them with the jus. Serve with seasonal vegetables.

PREPARATION TIME: 30 MINUTES | COOKING TIME: 2 HOURS 45 MINUTES | SERVES 4

ONE GIRL
AND HER COWS

BY HOLLY MOSCROP

"Both my mum and granny are also very passionate about cooking, especially with ingredients they've grown, reared or foraged. I was taught by them from a young age how much love and effort goes into our food, to always know and respect the origins of it and be proud of its story."

I was lucky enough to grow up on the beautiful Yorkshire farm I still get to call my home, immersed in the world of farming. A world I very quickly knew I never wanted to leave behind.

My grandfather began farming at Stockheld Grange Farm in the early 1960s, with my grandmother joining him here not long after. There were no livestock when she arrived, but she soon changed that and added some beef cows, some of the descendants of which we still have today, as well as sheep, pigs and chickens to make it a proper mixed farm like the one she'd grown up on.

My grandmother, or Granny to us grandchildren and our friends, is certainly where my initial love of livestock farming comes from. My childhood memories are filled with us tending to our small flock of sheep together, as well as her kitchen being home to hypothermic chicks, piglets and lambs that were warming up in the Aga. My dad also caught that love of livestock and despite not coming from a farming background, my mum was cut from that same cloth as well, so there wasn't really any chance of me wanting to do anything else!

Both my mum and granny are also very passionate about cooking, especially with ingredients they've grown, reared or foraged. I was taught by them from a young age how much love and effort goes into our food, to always know and respect the origins of it and be proud of its story.

My life didn't quite turn out as planned and my dreams of becoming a farmer and working alongside my dad had to be adapted when a debilitating long-term illness called M.E. came along and removed me from the life I once knew. But my love for British farming and our own farm remained ever strong, so in an attempt to find a way to stay connected to the world of agriculture and try reconnecting others to it too, I began writing a blog called One Girl and Her Cows.

My hope is to one day sell our own meat from our cattle through my website and give people the chance to know the whole story of the food on their plates, and how that food played a pivotal role in maintaining and protecting the British countryside we know and love.

HEDGEROW SPONGE PUDDING

This pudding is a celebration of the Great British Countryside and the fruits that nature delights us with. I made it with apples and blackberries because we were overrun with them, but you can swap the fruits for whatever you have a glut of; you really can't go wrong!

For the fruit filling

300g Bramley apples, fresh or frozen

250g blackberries, freshly foraged or frozen

2 tbsp cornflour

1 tbsp granulated sugar

For the sponge

250g self-raising flour (also works with gluten free self-raising flour)

50g British porridge oats (or rolled oats)

80g soft brown sugar

150g British unsalted butter, diced

2 medium British eggs

For the fruit filling

Preheat your oven to 180°c (160°c fan) and grease an 11-inch (28cm) baking dish. Peel, core and dice your apples before putting them into your dish with the blackberries (or any other berries you're using).

Sprinkle the cornflour and granulated sugar over the fruit, adding more sugar if you know the berries are particularly tart, and give it a quick stir. Place the dish of fruit in your preheated oven to bake for around 15 minutes while you make the sponge.

For the sponge

Place the flour, oats, soft brown sugar and butter into a bowl, or a food processor, and rub together, or pulse the processor, until the texture is like chunky breadcrumbs.

Remove around 4 heaped dessert spoons of the crumbly mixture and set aside in a separate bowl. Lightly beat the eggs in a mug and then stir them into the remaining mixture to create a smooth cake batter.

Remove your baked fruit from the oven and give it another stir to make sure all the pieces are spread evenly across the dish, then pour the sponge mixture over the fruit and smooth out the top.

Sprinkle the reserved crumble mixture over the top of the cake mix and return the dish to the oven for a further 30 to 45 minutes, or until lightly golden and a skewer comes out clean (this will vary depending on your oven).

Remove from the oven and allow the pudding to cool slightly (if you can wait) before scooping out generous portions and serving warm with cream, custard or vanilla ice cream. You can also pop leftovers into the fridge and reheat them the next day in the microwave. It's also rather moreish when eaten on its own, even when cold and straight from the fridge (not that I've stolen a spoonful, or two, when passing…) so enjoy!

PREPARATION TIME: 30 MINUTES | COOKING TIME: 40 MINUTES TO 1 HOUR | MAKES AN 11-INCH (28CM) ROUND PIE DISH

HUGH LOWE FARMS LTD

BY MARION REGAN

"Our summers are spent in a happy whirl of picking and packing delicious berries, keeping down the 'food miles' to the consumer. Our family know from long experience that the freshest home-grown berries taste the best."

Our family farming business, Hugh Lowe Farms, has always grown fruit in the Garden of England, and has specialised in berry growing since 1893, when my great-grandfather Bernard Champion planted his first field of strawberries. In those days local strawberry pickers were paid extra for each chip basket picked before seven o'clock in the morning, because these could be loaded on to a horse-drawn spring van and transported to the old Covent Garden market for sale that same day.

The farm is in the pretty village of Mereworth, on the free-draining soils of the Greensand Ridge, overlooking the Weald of Kent, in an area now also renowned for its vineyards. I took over from my father to become the fourth-generation farmer in Mereworth, having studied botany and ecology and worked for botanic gardens. Together with my husband Jon Regan, and daughter Amelia Mclean, I am passionate about sustainable berry production, and have long practised both 'sparing and sharing' our land with wildlife.

As a result, we have good populations of native pollinators such as solitary bees and hoverflies, and of farmland birds in our crops, as well as many wild areas on the farm that are rich in biodiversity. We are very open to innovation, searching for the latest, most flavourful varieties, and using biological methods to control pests and diseases wherever possible. By looking after our soil — so it locks up carbon from the air — and using renewable energy where possible, we are also driving down the carbon footprint of our fruit.

With a young and dynamic growing team, led by skilled grower Tom Pearson, we produce several thousand tonnes of strawberries, raspberries and blackberries each year. People come from many different countries to help harvest the fruit. Our summers are spent in a happy whirl of picking and packing delicious berries, keeping down the 'food miles' to the consumer. Our family know from long experience that the freshest home-grown berries taste the best. Our fruit can be found in many major supermarkets, local markets and farm shops. We are also proud to have provided all the strawberries served at the iconic Wimbledon Tennis Championships for nearly three decades!

ALISON'S AFTER SCHOOL STRAWBERRY FLAN

Growing up on a strawberry farm meant that summer teatime often revolved round a simple strawberry flan, scented with geranium leaves and piled high with home-grown strawberries and cream. My mother Alison made sure any leftovers were enjoyed by the family tortoise. I still make this today for visitors and look forward to my grandson enjoying it.

1-2 small, fresh, scented rose geranium leaves (optional)

110g butter, softened

110g caster sugar

2 large eggs (or 3 small)

1 tsp natural vanilla essence

110g self-raising flour

200-300ml whipping cream

400g-600g fresh English strawberries

Grease and line an 8" round loose-bottomed sandwich tin with baking paper and place the scented geranium leaves on the base if using. Preheat your oven to 170°c (150°c fan).

In a food mixer, beat together the butter and most of the sugar (keeping back a spoonful) for a full 5 minutes. In a separate bowl, lightly whisk the eggs with the vanilla essence. Add this egg mixture, bit by bit, to the butter and sugar, beating for another 5 minutes, then fold in the flour.

Spoon the mixture into the prepared tray and bake in the preheated oven for 35 minutes until a skewer comes out clean. Cool on a wire rack, then turn out on to a pretty platter. Gently peel away the baking paper and geranium leaves, then discard them.

Whip the cream to relatively firm peaks and spread it on top of the cooled cake base. Remove the green calyx from all the strawberries and arrange them, pointed end up, in close serried rows to completely cover the cake, slicing vertically if large. Dust with the remaining spoonful of caster sugar and arrange any leftover strawberries around the cake. Serve immediately, but leftovers are also delicious the next day.

PREPARATION TIME: 20 MINUTES | COOKING TIME: 35 MINUTES | SERVES 6-8

HUMBLE BY NATURE

· ·

BY TIM STEPHENS

"Giving people the opportunity to experience farm life when they come to Humble by Nature – learning animal husbandry, rural skills and crafts – has been an enjoyable and rewarding experience for me."

Born and brought up on a Welsh hill farm, I was always going to farm. Sarah and I tenant our 118-acre upland livestock farm in east Monmouthshire. We rent from Kate Humble and Ludo Graham, who set up Humble by Nature, a rural skills centre, on the farm.

We run 12 Hereford cross suckler cows and our calves are sold mainly as stores at around 12 months. Recently we've kept a few to finish as grass-reared and have been very pleased with the results. We run 240 breeding ewes, mainly Texels and mules with some Welsh. We also keep a small flock of Badger Face Welsh Mountain, a few Jacobs and rare breed Horned Dorsets. These breeds are great for hands-on experience for guests on our smallholding and sheep courses on the farm.

We currently have one Welsh, one Berkshire and one Oxford Sandy and Black sow. Sometimes we breed pure but we also use our Pietrain boar to produce a better carcass. Some of the weaners are sold locally, others are kept to finishing weight for local farm shops or for individuals. We always keep some for ourselves to make our own bacon and sausages, which is where the scotch egg recipe we have shared in this book came from. We were very pleased and a little surprised to win a first prize taste award with a joint from one of our Berkshire weaners.

Giving people the opportunity to experience farm life when they come to Humble by Nature – learning animal husbandry, rural skills and crafts – has been an enjoyable and rewarding experience for me. I reluctantly became a course tutor (teaching sheep, lambing and hedging courses) but this soon became something I looked forward to and a really enjoyable part of being on the farm. My favourite has to be hedge-laying as it is so rewarding to see the transformation from an overgrown, scruffy hedge to a beautiful work of art, enhancing the landscape and wildlife habitat, all completed by beginners.

I feel very passionate about local produce and keeping food miles low, while looking after the environment. Wales and the UK rear the best meat and grow the best food anyone could wish for, so please support your local producers!

FOR THE LOVE OF THE LAND II

· ·

PAGE 124

HUMBLE BY NATURE

RURAL SKILLS CENTRE

Compost Corner

PORK AND LEEK SCOTCH EGGS

I do love a scotch egg, so when I was asked to contribute a recipe it was the ideal opportunity to share my homemade version. Using our own free-range award-winning Berkshire sausage meat and free-range eggs, they are a delicious snack and surprisingly easy to make.

3 free-range eggs

1 thick slice of white bread (for breadcrumbs)

240g free-range Berkshire sausage meat

10g pork and leek sausage seasoning

A dusting of flour

Cooking oil (enough to cover your scotch eggs in the pan)

Bring a pan of water to the boil and boil 2 of the eggs for 5-6 minutes, depending on how runny you like your yolks. Crack the remaining egg into a bowl and whisk, then blitz the white bread into crumbs. Combine the sausage meat with the seasoning until well mixed.

Start to heat the oil slowly in a large, deep pan. When the boiled eggs are done, let them cool slightly before peeling off the shells. Roll out the seasoned sausage meat on a lightly floured board and form 2 oval shapes. Carefully wrap the peeled eggs in the sausage meat, making sure not to leave any gaps. Brush the scotch eggs with beaten egg and then roll in the breadcrumbs until coated.

Now test the oil temperature, either using a kitchen thermometer (the ideal temperature is 145°c) or by placing a small cube of bread in the oil which should brown in 45 seconds.

Once the oil has reached the required temperature, carefully place the scotch eggs into the pan and deep fry them for 7-8 minutes. This should give you a crispy golden egg with a slightly runny yolk.

Tip: Don't let your oil get too hot or the coating will burn and the meat will be undercooked. If you are worried about undercooking the scotch eggs, place them in a hot oven for a few minutes after frying.

I enjoy my scotch eggs best with a chunk of homemade bread, some strong cheese and my favourite pickle, or equally with homemade chunky chips.

JEKKA'S

BY JEKKA & ALISTAIR MCVICAR

"One of our three core roots is that we are environmentally conscious and for the past 35 years all the herbs grown at Jekka's have been raised using organic and sustainable principles, resulting in remarkable biodiversity at the herb farm."

Jekka's is a family-run herb farm with over 35 years' experience in growing and using medicinal and culinary herbs. At Jekka's we believe in cultivating flavour and aim to educate and inspire gardeners and cooks of all ages. We offer a variety of herb experiences from open days and private tours to master classes, corporate days and Jekka's HerbFest. These are all based around Jekka's Herbetum, a living encyclopaedia of over 400 culinary herbs, found at our herb farm in South Gloucestershire.

At Jekka's we strongly believe in promoting a sustainable and environmentally friendly approach to gardening that not only does you good but supports the natural ecosystem. One of our three core roots is that we are environmentally conscious and for the past 35 years all the herbs grown at Jekka's have been raised using organic and sustainable principles, resulting in remarkable biodiversity at the herb farm. We are proud of this diversity, from hoverflies to newts and a tremendous bumble bee population; there are now over 12 different species of bumble bee living at the herb farm.

Jekka herself has been awarded the Victoria Medal of Honour in Horticulture by the Royal Horticultural Society (RHS) as well as 62 RHS gold medals for her herb exhibits and is a Vice President of the RHS. She has written eight books, including Jekka's Complete Herb Book which has sold over a million copies worldwide. Jekka is well known for her herb expertise and designing herb gardens for hospitals, restaurants and private homes.

Alistair has been awarded a Ph.D. from the Grantham Institute of Climate Change, Imperial College London, as well as successfully achieving the Leith's Diploma in Food and Wine. He runs herb-based master classes at the herb farm.

JEKKA'S SUMMER HERB ROLLS

These rolls are a delicious snack, starter or canapé where herbs are the star. Add a selection of fresh herb leaves and herb flowers to make your own beautiful herb mosaic 'window' on the rice paper. They can be pre-made or assembled at the table which is enjoyable for adults and children alike.

For the pickled shallots

2 tsp black peppercorns

2 tsp coriander seeds

2 star anise

1 cinnamon stick

1 tsp Kosher salt

120ml white wine vinegar (or your herb vinegar)

350ml water

6 shallots or 1 red onion

For the summer rolls

30g beansprouts

2 large carrots, julienned

1 small cucumber, julienned

½ an avocado, sliced

½ cup mixed salad herb leaves including wild rocket (Diplotaxis tenuifolia), French sorrel (Rumex scutatus) and mizuna (Brassica rapa var. japonica) depending on availability, roughly chopped

Small bunch of Thai basil (Ocimum basilicum 'Horapha Nanum')

Small bunch of dill (Anethum graveolens)

Small bunch of spearmint (Mentha Spicata) or parsley (Petroselinum crispum 'French') depending on availability

12 rice paper wrappers

A few herb leaves, such as parsley (Petroselinum crispum 'French'), tree spinach (Chenopodium giganteum) and celery leaf (Apium graveolens)

A few herb flowers, such as garlic chives (Allium tuberosum), chicory (Cichorium intybus), thyme (Thymus vulgaris), oregano (Origanum vulgare) and coriander (Coriandrum sativum)

For the pickled shallots

Toast the peppercorns, coriander seeds, star anise and cinnamon in a dry frying pan on a medium heat until fragrant. Add the salt, vinegar and water then bring to the boil.

Peel and finely slice the shallots or onion into rings and place in a heatproof bowl. Using a sieve, strain the pickling liquid into the bowl, then leave to cool and let the flavours mingle.

If you have any pickled shallots leftover at the end of the meal, place the shallots and their pickling liquid in a jar and keep in the fridge for adding to salads and toasties.

For the summer rolls

Prepare all the vegetables and salad leaves, finely chop the herbs and then set all this to one side. Fill a large bowl with water in which to soften the rice paper. Don't soak the papers all at once; it's best to work with one at a time. They take about 10-30 seconds each (check the packet for times).

Soak one rice paper wrapper and then place a small bed of decorative herb leaves and flowers in the middle of the softened wrapper. Top with small amounts of every other ingredient. Although tempting, try not to over-fill the rolls as this will make them hard to roll up.

Roll the rice paper up around the filling, egg-roll style: pull the bottom up, fold the sides in, and roll tightly to close. Repeat the soaking, decorating, filling and rolling process until you have 12 rolls.

Serve your herb rolls with a selection of dipping sauces such as mushroom or peanut: for ideas and recipes see www.jekkas.com. Eat and enjoy!

JIMMY'S FARM
& WILDLIFE PARK

· ·

BY JIMMY DOHERTY

"Our first sow, Rosie, was so sweet she ended up living in the caravan with us – well, until she got too big! We worked every hour the day sent and created a tiny farm shop and butchery to sell our premium sausages and bacon."

I have always had a passion for wildlife. I worked at Mole Hall Wildlife Park in Saffron Walden when I was in my teens and loved taking care of a menagerie of different animals, from otters to chimpanzees, pigs to chinchillas: the dream began there. After a degree in zoology, I continued to study for a PHD in entomology. It was when I met my future wife, Michaela, that I decided to give it all up and train as a pig farmer.

The Essex Pig Company in Suffolk was born shortly afterwards on a derelict farm that housed our very first rare breed, Essex Pigs. Sustainability was at the heart of everything we did as our herd munched on acorns and matured in 100 acres of ancient woodland. It was weirdly romantic, like someone had stopped time. We lived in a tiny caravan and started to build up our breeding stock. Our first sow, Rosie, was so sweet she ended up living in the caravan with us – well, until she got too big! We worked every hour the day sent and created a tiny farm shop and butchery to sell our premium sausages and bacon.

The BBC took an interest in our little story and followed our endeavours to breathe life back into this almost extinct breed. Quality meat and food production was at the heart of our operation and soon we developed the derelict barns into a series of shops and a farm restaurant. The restaurant now relies solely on our farm-produced meat, from beef and lamb to all our pork dishes. We're quite famous for our sausage rolls and can sell as many as 10,000 a month in the busy summer period!

The farm has slowly developed and my childhood dream of owning a wildlife park has certainly come true. We now have over 90 different species of domestic and exotic livestock! In 2016 I was honoured to become the youngest President of the Rare Breeds Survival Trust (RBST). The trust is very important to me as they ensure we do not lose the diversity and importance of our native breeds. In July 2021 we became the first recipient of the RBST Rare Breeds Approved Associate Accreditation. I hope that our farm continues to represent our great British rare breeds and that, by working with the RBST, we can help other farms, zoos and wildlife parks across the country to do the same.

CRISPY PORK BELLY, BRAISED HISPI AND JUNIPER

. . . .

I absolutely love this delicious recipe. If you can, I recommend getting the pork belly from a local butcher. You will be able to tell the difference in the meat; its rich variety of flavour comes from a good life, and you'll be supporting local farmers just like me.

1kg pork belly, skin on

50ml gin

2 tbsp juniper berries

1 tbsp rock salt (we use Maldon)

1 tbsp black pepper

1 lime, zested

30ml rapeseed oil

1 hispi cabbage

50g butter

300ml vegetable stock

200ml pork stock

100ml double cream

1 tbsp cornflour

Preheat the oven to 130°c. Score the skin of the pork belly, place it in a tray, and pour over the gin. Crush the juniper berries, rock salt and black pepper, then rub this mixture into the skin with the lime zest and rapeseed oil. Place the pork in the preheated oven for 1 hour 30 minutes. Cooking it slowly allows the fat to render and keep the meat soft, while the skin will be crisp.

Meanwhile, remove the outer leaves of the cabbage and cut it into quarters, ensuring the root remains intact as this will hold it together. Fry both sides of the cabbage in pan with a little oil and butter on a medium heat until they have a nice colour, then transfer to a tray and pour in the vegetable stock. Place the tray in the oven to cook for 20 minutes until soft.

After the pork has been in for 90 minutes, turn the oven up to 190°c and continue cooking for 30 minutes to crisp up the skin. Remove the pork belly from the tray, pour off any excess fat, add the pork stock and heat gently to loosen up the juices. Stir in the cream and cornflour, then bring to the boil and simmer for 2 minutes.

Cut the pork belly into 4 pieces with a serrated knife, then drizzle with the creamy sauce, avoiding the crackling as you'll want it to stay crisp. Serve with the cabbage and your favourite potatoes (I prefer a fondant or bubble and squeak). A good piece of meat will always speak for itself, and only needs a simple accompaniment to make it shine.

PREPARATION TIME: 30 MINUTES | COOKING TIME: 2 HOURS | SERVES 4

KNEPP WILD RANGE MEAT

BY CHARLIE BURRELL

"I embarked on an experiment to see if we could use free-roaming herbivores to generate habitat for wildlife on our depleted, polluted land. We introduced sturdy old breeds of domestic livestock to mimic the actions of the ancient herds that would once have roamed Britain."

In 1999 I made the life-changing decision to give up arable and dairy farming on our 3,500 acres of heavy Sussex clay. We rarely made a profit and were heavily in debt. I decided to do something that would work with nature, rather than battling against it.

That's when I hit upon rewilding and embarked on an experiment to see if we could use free-roaming herbivores to generate habitat for wildlife on our depleted, polluted land. We introduced sturdy old breeds of domestic livestock to mimic the actions of the ancient herds that would once have roamed Britain. Old English longhorns stand in as proxies of their ancestor, the extinct aurochs. Exmoor ponies imitate the tarpan. Tamworth pigs do the job of wild boar. Red and fallow deer add to the mix.

The disturbances of these animals – trampling, rootling, wallowing, browsing, grazing and dispersing seeds in different ways – has proved to be rocket-fuel for biodiversity. Their dung – organic, of course, because we no longer use wormers or antibiotics – has helped restore our soil. We keep the stocking density very low to encourage vegetation complexity but also to ensure the animals come through the harshest winter in good shape. Because they eat what they like – we don't supplementary feed them – the animals are incredibly healthy, benefiting from a smorgasbord of native herbs, grasses and foliage. They self-medicate, nibbling sallow as an anti-inflammatory or nettles to replenish iron.

This means that, in stark contrast to intensive grain-fed systems, our animals put down fats that are high in Omega 3, conjugated linoleic acid (which fights cancer and diabetes), vitamins E and B, calcium, magnesium and potassium which are vital for human health. A balanced number of grazing animals also means the soil and vegetation continues to be positively stimulated to store carbon.

Our wonderful manager Ian Mepham ensures the processing, packaging and delivery of our meat is sustainable and low-carbon. Dry-aging and butchery take place on site and our CUBO2 Smart refrigeration system – the largest in independent use in the UK – replaces conventional harmful refrigerants. We're avid proponents of nose-to-tail eating and our cowhides make leather furniture designed by Bill Amberg.

I'm thrilled that the Independent chose us as Best Meat Box two years running and Delicious Magazine considers us one of the best meat delivery services. But most of all, I'm proud that the way we produce meat at Knepp is good for human health, good for the animals, and good for the planet.

RACK OF VENISON AND VENISON CHORIZO
WITH WARM WINTER SALAD
···

This is a simple but indulgent dish, great for a hearty family meal or a real showstopper for a dinner party. Serve the venison with a seasonal salad to suit the time of year (for spring and summer the winter salad can be replaced by a charred lettuce or a mix of leafy vegetables with a dressing).

For the venison chorizo

1kg organic venison mince

3 cloves of garlic, crushed

50g smoked paprika

20g chipotle chilli flakes

20g salt

For the rack of venison

1 x 4-bone rack of organic venison

Salt and pepper

For the warm winter salad

2 large Maris Piper or other roasting potatoes, peeled and cut into 1-inch pieces

2 turnips, cut into 1-inch cubes

2 parsnips, halved lengthways and cut into ½ inch batons

2 red onions, cut into 8 wedges each

3 large carrots, halved lengthways and cut into 1-inch pieces

½ butternut squash, halved lengthways and sliced into ½ inch semicircles

1 large sweet potato, cut into 1-inch cubes

1 medium-sized fennel bulb, halved lengthways and sliced into ½ inch slices

6 cloves of garlic, peeled and lightly crushed

3 sprigs of thyme

2 sprigs of sage

2 sprigs of rosemary

Olive oil

For the venison chorizo

First, preheat your oven to 230°c or Gas Mark 8 as you'll need it later. Combine the venison mince with the garlic and seasoning in a large bowl and mix thoroughly until everything is a gorgeous deep orange colour. With damp hands, portion the mix into 8 equal pieces and roughly shape into sausages. Transfer the chorizo to a tray and keep in the fridge until needed.

For the rack of venison

Lightly score the fat on the venison rack (without cutting into the meat) to create little diamond shapes, then season with a little salt and pepper.

For the warm winter salad

Put the potatoes into a saucepan and just cover with water, bring to the boil and then drain well. Put the par-boiled potatoes into a deep roasting tray with all the other vegetables except the fennel. Massage 2 tablespoons of olive oil into the vegetables and season with salt and pepper, then put the tray into your preheated oven and set a timer for 30 minutes.

When the timer goes off, check that the vegetables are almost cooked, then add the fennel, garlic, thyme, sage and rosemary. Place the tray back in the oven and set the timer for 20 minutes.

To cook the venison

Heat a large frying pan without any oil and when it is searing hot, add your prepared venison rack fat side down to sear until well browned. Repeat on each side, then place on the second shelf of your hot oven for 10 minutes.

Put the same frying pan (leaving the venison fat in) on a medium heat and then place your chorizo sausages gently into the hot pan. Lightly press each sausage until it has 2 flat sides and cook for 5 minutes on each side. Put the pan to one side for the dressing.

Once you have turned the chorizo sausages for the first time, take your rack of venison out the oven and place somewhere warm to rest.

To serve

Share the roasted vegetables between 4 plates, heaping them in the middle and removing any herb sprigs. Slice the venison rack between each bone, then place a piece on each plate, gently resting against the vegetables. Cut each chorizo sausage into 3 pieces and scatter 6 pieces onto each plate around the vegetables. Finally, put 3 tablespoons of olive oil in the pan used to cook the venison and chorizo and warm slightly. Drizzle this over the dish as a dressing and serve. Enjoy!

PREPARATION TIME: 30 MINUTES | COOKING TIME: 50 MINUTES | SERVES 4

L'ENCLUME

BY SIMON ROGAN

"The farm is an extension of our kitchen, and everyone gets involved, working side by side with the farmers to develop a complete understanding of our ingredients. There's nothing like sowing a seed and seeing it all the way through to the plate."

At L'Enclume, everything is based around the incredible ingredients we grow on Our Farm, situated less than a mile away in Cumbria's beautiful Cartmel Valley. When I first set up my flagship restaurant here, we had some difficulties with the quality and availability of fresh produce in the area. Those frustrations became the reason we established a farm, in order to provide the kitchen with natural produce that was fresher and better than anything we could buy.

For me and my chefs, this produce is absolutely the driving force behind everything we do. The farm is an extension of our kitchen, and everyone gets involved, working side by side with the farmers to develop a complete understanding of our ingredients. There's nothing like sowing a seed and seeing it all the way through to the plate; this a huge part of why we all love what we do here. Because we grow everything ourselves, there is total control over the quality of our supply at L'Enclume. This also means that our menu changes constantly to showcase what's best, making vegetables the stars of the show. My cooking style has altered over the years to reflect this balance and highlight the natural tastes, textures and fragrances of our produce.

We know what grows best in our harsh Cumbrian winters and fruitful summers, so the ingredients which excel in our climate are those which connect us to our surroundings. Seasonal food is just one part of our ethos on sustainability, which we are hugely proud of, especially as we have two green Michelin stars across two continents.

This ethos also feeds into two new initiatives that we developed recently in response to challenging circumstances for both farming and hospitality, which I'm very excited about. We have continued the 'at home' service that began during lockdown, working from dedicated facilities to deliver our restaurant meals around the UK, sourcing ingredients and packaging as locally as possible, utilising wool inserts to keep the produce cool, as well as creating a number of local jobs. We have also begun training young people ourselves through a joint initiative with Kendal College, called the Academy by Simon Rogan, and our aim is to motivate them to stay in this industry that has so much to offer when we do it right.

Photos by Cristian Barnett www.cristianbarnett.com

ZAINO COURGETTES CARAMELISED IN YEAST AND FENNEL POLLEN WITH PICKLED QUAILS EGGS, COURGETTE FLOWER FRITTERS AND AROMATIC SUMMER HERBS

··

We believe that Zaino courgettes, a variety that we grow on Our Farm located in the Cartmel Valley, are the best you will ever taste, especially roasted in yeast and fennel pollen butter. We grow masses of fennel plants too, mainly to collect their amazing pollen but also to make fennel top vinegar for pickling.

40g unsalted butter

0.7g yeast flakes

1.4g fennel pollen

400g Zaino courgettes, deseeded and diced

500ml sunflower oil

Salt, to taste

50g egg yolk

1 tsp English mustard

200g rice flour

200g sparkling water

4 Zaino courgette flowers

200ml white wine vinegar

200g fennel tops

4 quails eggs

Aromatic herbs and flowers, to garnish (such as fennel fronds, amaranth, chickweed, oxalis, borage, dianthus, marigold)

Soften the unsalted butter while you toast the yeast flakes for a minute or two in a non-stick pan with a touch of vegetable oil until golden. Chill the toasted yeast, then combine it with the softened butter and fennel pollen, roll in cling film and chill the butter in the fridge to set hard overnight.

Roast the diced courgettes in a large pan on a medium heat with the sunflower oil for 10-15 minutes until lightly golden. At this stage, strain the courgette oil and place it in the fridge, return the courgettes to the pan, then add the yeast and fennel pollen butter and cook for another 8-10 minutes to caramelise them further. Season with salt.

To make a courgette emulsion, whisk the egg yolk with the English mustard and 250ml of the reserved chilled courgette oil until thick and thoroughly combined.

Make the batter for the fritters by mixing the rice flour with the sparkling water until smooth, then tear the courgette flowers into pieces. Dip them in the batter and then deep fry at 180°c for 4-5 minutes until golden brown. Season immediately with salt and leave to drain.

To pickle the quails eggs, bring the white wine vinegar to the boil in a small pan, add the fennel tops and then leave to rest overnight. The next day, sieve the vinegar and add 100g of water.

Crack the eggs and separate the whites from the yolks. Immerse the yolks in the fennel-infused pickling liquid for at least 1 hour before serving. Make a few extra to allow for breakages, as they are very delicate!

To serve

Place 50g of the roasted courgette mix in a circle in the centre of each plate. Make a hole in the middle of the circle, pipe a nice dot of courgette emulsion into it and then place the pickled egg yolk on top of the emulsion. Break the crispy courgette flowers into 2-3cm pieces and arrange these on top of the diced courgette. Dress with the aromatic summer herbs, placing them around the quails egg and on top of the crispy flowers.

PREPARATION TIME: 1 HOUR, PLUS OVERNIGHT FOR THE FENNEL TOP PICKLE AND THE BUTTER
| COOKING TIME: 10 MINUTES | SERVES 4

MALT COAST BREWERY

BY BRUIN MAUFE

"We grow a heritage variety of winter barley called Maris Otter. This is delivered to the local floor maltings in relatively small batches and returned to the farm where it is crushed on site: a genuine grain to glass story."

Our family farm is based within the Holkham Estate on the beautiful North Norfolk Coast. We have been growing prime malting barley here for generations. With the sandy loam over chalk and coastal climate, it really is one of the best locations in the UK for growing malting barley. So, it made perfect sense to focus on this special crop when my brother and I were looking at ways to move back to the farm from London and help to diversify the business and ensure its survival.

We founded Malt Coast in 2017, a craft brewery which uses the farm's award-winning barley to brew beers with a focus on traceability and provenance. We grow a heritage variety of winter barley called Maris Otter. This is delivered to the local floor maltings in relatively small batches and returned to the farm where it is crushed on site: a genuine grain to glass story. It was important to us that the diversification clearly aligned with the farm and it's exciting to be using our barley to brew these unique beers.

The beer is sold in The Real Ale Shop on the farm itself as well as pubs, restaurants, delis, and cafés across the local area, plus some of the country's leading restaurants in London. It's very much a family business that draws on our local heritage. As UK farming undergoes many changes over the coming years with some significant challenges, the farm is likely to further rely on these diversified sources of income.

We also have a responsibility to preserve this wonderful place for future generations and to this end we have placed 20% of the land into environmental schemes. It is our hope that the natural environment and agricultural business can flourish together.

CHOCALE PUDDING

I love chocolate and I love beer, and this recipe brings the two together to great effect. A chocolate pudding with unusual contrasting textures of a luscious sponge over a warm rich sauce.

For the pudding

50g butter

3 level tbsp cocoa

75g caster sugar

125g self-raising flour

Pinch of salt

6 tbsp milk

¼ tsp vanilla essence

For the topping

100g dark brown sugar

2 level tbsp cocoa

330ml Malt Coast Black IPA (or a dark stout/porter)

Icing sugar, for dusting

Cream or vanilla ice cream, to serve

For the pudding

Gently heat the butter in a saucepan until melted but not browned. Mix in the cocoa powder and the sugar. Sift the flour and salt into a bowl together, then gently beat in the butter mixture along with the milk and vanilla essence. Turn the mixture into a shallow, greased ovenproof dish approximately 23cm (9 inches) in diameter.

For the topping

Mix the brown sugar and cocoa powder together, then sprinkle over the pudding. Pour all the beer over the top.

Bake the pudding in a preheated oven at 180°c (Gas Mark 4) for 30-40 minutes, or until the top springs back when lightly pressed but the sauce remains liquid beneath.

Dust the pudding with icing sugar and serve warm with cream or vanilla ice cream.

PREPARATION TIME: 15 MINUTES | COOKING TIME: 30-40 MINUTES | SERVES 6

MILLBANK FARM

BY EMILY MCGOWAN

"With this most recent diversification into serving the local public, we see the importance of always evolving and moving positively with the times. Our effort was to create a customer experience that provides fresh, honest, seriously local produce with as little plastic packaging as possible."

Millbank Farm has existed on the same site in Killinchy since 1889 and while a lot has changed over the decades, we have continued to produce great quality food in the fields of County Down for six generations and counting. In the early years, the farm was a corn and sutch mill which processed flax for the local linen trade, but today we are a medium mixed farm of around 400 acres, including 80 acres of cereals and 80 acres of veg, as well as grazing for dairy heifers and 200 ewes. We also have two broiler houses for supply of Moy Park chicken, and an exciting development in recent years was opening the farm's first customer-facing venture: Millbank Farm Shop, in pride of place on Saintfield's high street.

With this most recent diversification into serving the local public, we see the importance of always evolving and moving positively with the times. Our effort was to create a customer experience that provides fresh, honest, seriously local produce – mostly grown at home on our farm or in the immediate area – with as little plastic packaging as possible. The shop provides an ever-changing variety of fresh fruit, vegetables, dairy and whole foods, perfect for the home cook and chefs alike. Quality, seasonality and a love of good food is at the forefront of everything we do.

My father Adrian is at the helm of the business, with three daughters raised together with my mum Paddy. My eldest sister Susie is a graphic designer in London and my middle sister Victoria is a teacher at the local primary school, while I've recently joined Dad on the farm in Killinchy. The family business is exactly that, with everyone adding their own skills and input to make the legacy of Millbank Farm a success.

As a business we are committed to farming sustainably. We work the land in a sympathetic way and take every opportunity to enhance the local biodiversity of the countryside. Some of our environmental initiatives include tree planting, seeding wildflowers and keeping livestock to create higher organic matter in the soils. Our awards include one for 'future proofing' from Waitrose and McDonalds Outstanding Farmer of the Year, both in 2019, as well as two for diversification in 2021 which we are very proud to have recognised.

SEASONAL SUPERFOOD SALAD

This versatile crowd pleaser is crunchy, nutty and nourishing. It's a cracking recipe for packing in many varieties of vegetables, depending on the seasons and what's available to you!

250g baby beetroot

200g quinoa

100g wild rice

400g Puy lentils

400g chickpeas

1 bulb of fennel

100g kale

15g flat leaf parsley

15g mint

1 tbsp white wine vinegar

2 tbsp extra virgin olive oil

Sea salt and black pepper

2 ripe avocados

100g purple sprouting broccoli

150g cottage cheese

4 tsp harissa paste

50g mixed seeds (pumpkin, sunflower, etc.)

1 pomegranate, for the seeds

100g feta, crumbled

Scrub the beetroot bulbs, parboil until soft, then peel and quarter. Cook the grains in salted boiling water until tender, then drain.

In a large bowl, toss the cooked quinoa, rice, lentils, chickpeas and beetroot together. Shred the fennel and kale, then add them to the bowl.

Finely chop the parsley and mint, then add them to the bowl along with the vinegar, oil, a pinch of sea salt and black pepper to taste. Toss everything together.

Put a griddle pan on a high heat while you halve, peel and destone the avocados. Grill them cut side down in the hot pan for 5 minutes until bar marked.

Meanwhile, blanch the purple sprouting broccoli in salted boiling water for 4 minutes, then drain well.

To serve

Divide the dressed salad mix between 4 serving bowls. Place the grilled avocado halves on top, fill the hollows where the stones were with the cottage cheese, then top with the purple sprouting broccoli. Spoon over the harissa and scatter the mixed seeds on top. Finally, finish the salad with the pomegranate seeds and crumbled feta.

Tips

Buy vacuum-packed beetroot and packets of cooked grain for convenience if you're short of time. Alter the greens you use depending on what is in season, and serve the salad with poached chicken for extra protein if you like.

PERSON & FREIRE LTD

· ·

BY JOE FREIRE

"My success as a grower has helped to build the trust of my customers, who appreciate my produce. This is very important to me and of course to my team of staff, who play a big role in keeping our standards high."

The best thing about my job is the freedom to be on the fields and working on the land, as this is very satisfying and rewarding. Give me a tractor over a computer any day. Farming provides a great environment and plenty of opportunity for diversity. I love the process of sowing a little seed and in a short time seeing it develop to maturity, then being able to harvest it.

I was born in Madeira and moved to Jersey just after I left school in 1981. After working a few agriculture seasons on different farms, I took employment with Mr. Theodor Person at La Hougette Farm, in St. Lawrence, where he grew strawberries, paeonies and vegetables. Some time later, I married Mr Person's eldest daughter and we had three beautiful children.

In 1984, just before my then father-in-law retired, we formed Person & Freire Limited, specialising in farming good quality produce such as strawberries (which I am known for) and raspberries, asparagus, rhubarb and anemones. The strawberries became so popular that I had to employ more staff to keep up with the local market demand.

In 2016, as part of my ethos of always experimenting with new crops, I bought 100 commercial lemon trees which are now in full production, making me the only person on the island to grow and sell this variety of citrus. Today, my produce is on sale across multiple stores, including the local Co-op, central market, wholesalers, farmers' markets and at my own roadside stall in St. Lawrence.

My success as a grower has helped to build the trust of my customers, who appreciate my produce. This is very important to me and of course to my team of staff, who play a big role in keeping our standards high. I take great pride in growing fruit and vegetables for the local population in Jersey, keeping the carbon footprint of my business very low by avoiding long distance transportation and providing fresh produce grown on the island with care. Our secret is the soul of the business!

LEMON TART

Lemons have been part of my daily diet for many years and therefore I use lemons in many different ways for drinks, food and desserts. The leaves can be used to make a fresh infusion, the juice enhances so many foods and is also an antiseptic, while a squeezed lemon can be used for combatting odours in the kitchen sink!

For the pastry

200g plain flour

180g butter

100g sugar

Pinch of salt

1 lemon, zested

2 eggs, beaten

For the filling

100g butter

100g sugar

3 eggs

4 lemons, zested

150g ground almonds

Pinch of salt

For the pastry

Rub the flour and butter together in a large bowl until the mixture looks like breadcrumbs. Stir in the sugar, salt and lemon zest before gradually adding the beaten egg to bind the mixture together. Bring the pastry into a smooth ball, wrap it in cling film and place in the fridge to chill for 30 minutes.

Once chilled, roll out the pastry on a clean surface dusted with flour to match the size of your tart tin. Gently lay the pastry sheet over the tin and mould it to the base, being careful not to make any holes. Prick the pastry base with a fork and place back in the fridge while you make the filling.

For the filling

Preheat the oven to 160°c. In a bowl, beat the butter and sugar together, then add the eggs and mix until well combined. Do the same with the lemon zest, ground almonds and salt until smooth.

Pour the filling into the prepared pastry case so it almost reaches the top but doesn't spill over, as this will make the pastry stick to the tin. Slice one of the lemons you zested earlier very thinly, then lay the slices on top of the filling.

Bake the tart in the preheated oven for 30 minutes. Let it cool, then sift some icing sugar over the top to decorate, cut into slices and enjoy.

PREPARATION TIME: 15 MINUTES | COOKING TIME: 30 MINUTES | SERVES 4-6

SHIMPLING PARK FARM

BY JOHN AND ALICE PAWSEY

"Although organic farming is seen by some as a return to an older style, we have pioneered a system that is gentler on nature and our soils by using modern technology to guide our machinery in treading lightly on our fields, and precisely weeding our crops using robotics."

We have been farming in Suffolk for four generations and in 1999 converted the farm to organic production due to increasing concerns about nature loss and soil degradation on the farm. Farming without the use of pesticides or artificial fertilisers means that we need a very long and diverse rotation, which is very exciting as we have to grow lots and lots of different crops. These include quinoa, chia, spelt, heritage wheats for speciality breadmaking and oats for breakfast cereals.

Avoiding artificial fertilisers means that we have to feed our soils naturally by growing herbal fertility leys with lots of clover in them. This not only builds organic matter and sequesters carbon but also provides nutrients for our growing crops as well as grazing for our 1,000 Romney ewes and their lambs, which we reintroduced onto the farm in 2015. All our sheep graze outside for 365 days of the year, and we picked the Romney ewe as they can lamb outside without interference. Having animals on the farm is good for our soils and wildlife, plus it's wonderful to see a changing landscape as they move around our farm within the rotation.

Although organic farming is seen by some as a return to an older style, we have pioneered a system that is gentler on nature and our soils by using modern technology to guide our machinery in treading lightly on our fields, and precisely weeding our crops using robotics. Over the last 20 years we have managed to halt, and in some cases reverse, the decline in farmland birds as well as seeing species of pollinators and pond dwellers never before found in Suffolk. We have a close relationship with The Suffolk Wildlife Trust who do all our nature surveys.

But we still have more to do. In 2020, we planted 50 acres of agroforestry (cropping around lines of trees with the aim of drawing species into the fields and helping them move between woodlands) and have also started restoring and rediscovering our old farm ponds. None of this would be possible without our enthusiastic team who are constantly up for a challenge! Our arable team are instrumental in growing our crops, while our shepherds make sure that our sheep and lambs are raised to the highest welfare standards. I hope that you can taste the difference in our clover-fed lambs!

BUTTERFLIED SUMMER LAMB

Our clover-fed lamb is cooked with summer ingredients over native wood in this recipe, creating a zingy and tender dish that's perfect for warmer weather.

1 leg of lamb, butterflied

4 shallots or 2 onions

4 tinned anchovies

4 cloves of garlic

Fresh tarragon

1 lemon

Sea salt

Fresh coarsely ground black pepper

Either butterfly the lamb leg yourself or buy it already prepared, but make sure that the meat is of an even depth. Score the meat diagonally across the grain at about 1cm, depending on thickness.

To make the marinade, finely chop the shallots or onions and the anchovies until the latter is almost a paste. Crush the garlic cloves with the skin on, roughly chop the fresh tarragon and squeeze the lemon juice into a bowl. Roughly chop the lemon skin and place into the bowl along with the prepared ingredients, adding salt and pepper to taste. With both hands, thoroughly mix and knead the mixture to get all the flavours working together. Pour the marinade into a recycled plastic bag, add the butterflied leg and knead the marinade into the meat. Tie a knot in the bag to seal.

Light your barbecue with a stack of thinly split native hardwood and let the flames die down before cooking. While you wait, return to the marinating lamb and knead the mixture again into the meat. Repeat this occasionally until the barbecue is ready.

Once the flames have died down, barbecue the butterflied lamb for 20 minutes, turning it regularly, and apply some of the marinade after each turn. Don't worry if the outside of the lamb blackens due to the flames, it all adds to the flavour! When the cooking time is up, cut into the meat to check it is done to your taste, or use a meat thermometer.

If you like your lamb less rare, extend your cooking time but remove it from any remaining flames.

Serve with baked potatoes or potato wedges, young broad beans, summer salad and a juicy red wine.

PREPARATION TIME: 30 MINUTES | COOKING TIME: 20 MINUTES | SERVES 8

SITOPIA FARM

· ·

BY CHLOË DUNNETT (FOUNDER AND CHIEF GROWER)

"As a social enterprise we are on a mission to improve the food system. For us that means a world where the food we grow and eat nourishes both people and planet."

We are a modern, urban farm growing delicious fresh vegetables, fruit and flowers in Greenwich, inner London. As a social enterprise we are on a mission to improve the food system. For us that means a world where the food we grow and eat nourishes both people and planet. Sitopia means 'the food place' and is a phrase coined by Carolyn Steel, author of Sitopia and one of our wonderful advisory board members.

I'm new to farming, having switched careers a few years ago to pursue a long-held dream. An MSc in food policy, an urban food growing traineeship with Growing Communities, and leaving London to work on others' farms followed. Lockdown (and falling in love!) took me back to the big city and I was determined to set up a farm here, where I knew more were needed. Initially we started on two small sites and then in March 2021 expanded into a more permanent two acre site, generously loaned to us by the Woodlands Farm Trust. 400 backers for our Crowdfunder, nearly 300 local volunteers, and a lot of sweat, magic, grit and tears meant that in just a few months we converted our ex-pasture field into a working small horticultural farm producing and selling good food.

We use organic regenerative agricultural techniques, building the soil's fertility and growing healthy, strong, nutritious plants through the use of organic composts, natural fertilisers and 'no-dig' methods which preserve and enhance the structure and biology of the soil. We want to build a circular economy, using Londoners' recycled green waste, local woodchip and food waste which we recycle into our compost. A diverse selection of crops enables us to provide a wide variety of tasty produce and maximises resilience, productivity and biodiversity on our farm. Selling locally benefits our community by delivering fresh produce, often harvested on the same day, and reducing food miles.

We also work with hundreds of local volunteers, open up the farm to visitors to help increase city dwellers' understanding of food production, host school visits, offer discounts on our weekly produce bags to those on lower incomes and donate food to local community projects. Ultimately though, we don't believe the answer is cheaper food: cheap food is a myth, with the environmental, health or social costs being picked up by someone somewhere. We need system change to ensure good food is more widely accessible through measures like subsidies, taxation and proper Living Wages. In the meantime, we want to show just how quickly more of London's land could be converted into healthy, environmentally friendly, community-engaged food production.

TOMATO AND SPINACH LASAGNE
(RECIPE BY ED NASSAU LAKE)

I'm lucky enough to share my home and life with Ed, who was a chef before turning his hand to antiquarian bookselling so our flat is always full of delicious cooking smells. This is from our lockdown cookbook, inspired by Sitopia Farm produce. The spinach can be substituted with kale, cavolo nero or chard.

For the tomato sauce

Olive or rapeseed oil

2 large onions (preferably red), finely diced

1 large carrot, finely diced

6 cloves of garlic, finely sliced

8 sprigs of thyme, leaves finely chopped

3 large bay leaves (fresh if available, or dried)

1.5kg tomatoes, roughly chopped

2 tbsp tomato purée

1 small bunch of basil

Salt and pepper

For the filling

800g spinach

250g parmesan, grated

200g soft ricotta

½ lemon, zested and juiced

400g lasagne sheets

For the bechamel sauce

85g butter

75g flour

800ml milk

Nutmeg

For the tomato sauce

Heat a generous glug of olive or rapeseed oil in a heavy-based saucepan. Add the onion, carrot, garlic, thyme and bay leaves with a large pinch of salt. Sweat with the lid on over a low heat until soft (but not browned). Add the tomatoes and tomato purée, increase the heat and allow the tomatoes to collapse and the sauce to come to the boil. Stir, reduce the heat, then simmer until thickened. This will take about 20 minutes. Take off the heat and roughly tear in the basil. Blitz into a smooth sauce or leave as it is, then season to taste and set aside.

For the filling

Meanwhile, in another pan, melt a generous knob of butter and gently wilt the spinach with the lid on until cooked. Transfer to a colander to drain. When cooled, gently squeeze off any excess liquid. In a bowl, mix 100g of the parmesan with the ricotta, lemon zest and lemon juice, then fold in the drained spinach.

For the bechamel sauce

In a heavy-based pan, gently melt the butter before adding the flour. Stir gently for a minute or two without letting the mixture brown. Turn up the heat slightly and add a glug of the milk, stirring constantly. Once the milk has been incorporated, add another glug. Repeat until all the milk has been incorporated, leaving you with a silky smooth white sauce the consistency of thick double cream. Season with a pinch of salt and a light grating of nutmeg.

Now to assemble the lasagne. Place a single layer of pasta sheets into the bottom of your baking dish. Add a layer of tomato sauce, followed by a layer of bechamel sauce and half the spinach filling. Repeat. Add a final layer of lasagne sheets and bechamel, then grate the remaining parmesan over the top. You can now keep the lasagne in the fridge or freezer until you need it, or cook it fresh. Bake in a preheated oven at 180°c until light brown and bubbling on top (approximately 30-40 minutes).

We like to eat this with one of our Sitopia Farm salad mixes, which change each week and often contain edible flowers for a pleasing twist on the plate and palate.

PREPARATION TIME: 45 MINUTES | COOKING TIME: 40 MINUTES | SERVES 6-8

VILLAGE FARM

BY TOM & LISA MARTIN

"Whether we realise it or not, the whole agricultural landscape across the UK is inextricably linked."

One of the things we're passionate about on our mixed pasture and arable farm is helping people to see what happens on the other side of the farm gate, and here in the UK we can be proud of our world-leading standards in animal welfare, food provenance, and environmental protection. That doesn't mean we're resting on our laurels, or passing up opportunities to continuously improve, but we should recognise where we are.

Whether we realise it or not, the whole agricultural landscape across the UK is inextricably linked. Straw from our farm provides winter bedding for my neighbour's cattle, who are fed on reject or rotten potatoes and carrots or other 'waste' from vegetable production, and in turn their manure – a mixture of dung, urine, and straw – makes the best fertiliser nature can provide for our arable plants. Our wheat and barley, though mainly destined for bread-making and distilling, sometimes fail to make the highest grade, yet there is always a market as the grains can still feed chickens or pigs. In many cases the waste from chickens and pigs, as well as other agricultural enterprises such as UK sugar production, is fed into anaerobic digesters to produce green energy (with the leftover 'digestate' making an excellent plant feed for our crop), and sometimes the heat produced by these anaerobic digesters is used to heat greenhouses for year-round production of tomatoes, salad crops, or fruit. Nature never wastes anything, and modern UK farmers try to emulate her as best we can.

Throughout the summer months we collect delicious, locally grown fruits starting with early strawberries and raspberries from the allotment; tayberries, redcurrants and blackcurrants from our neighbouring 'pick-your-own' farm; not forgetting mouth-watering blueberries from nearby growers; and finishing with hedgerow blackberries picked at their tangiest in September. We call these 'forageberries' and any that aren't eaten fresh (or in many cases on the spot!) are sent to the freezer to be summoned for winter crumbles, or a sumptuous meringue pudding like the recipe we have shared in this book.

A recent resolution of ours is to never pass a sign that says 'Eggs for Sale' in order to support small-scale and local producers while encouraging the work that free-ranging farmed poultry do in feasting on grubs, insects, and seeds much as their avian relations do in the wild. When we combine all these delicious ingredients with British sugar (the imported stuff needs more acres to grow the same amount) which travels on average just 168 miles from field to wholesale, you can bake up a celebration of British summer and a taste of heaven.

© Lisa Miosi

VILLAGE FARM

Photo © Lisa Miosi

FORAGEBERRY MERINGUE

· ·

British farming is a world-leading and diverse industry; it's something that we can really be proud of. This simple recipe combines some of those delicious ingredients for a celebration of British produce. To those who haven't tried making meringue before, it's easier than you think.

Foraged berries (raspberries, strawberries, redcurrants, blackcurrants, tayberries or similar)

3 large eggs (or 4 small ones)

180g caster sugar

Icing sugar, to dust

Sprigs of fresh mint

Preheat the oven to 140°c or 120°c fan, and line a baking tray with greaseproof paper. Pop the foraged berries in the freezer. If you can't find wild growing fruit, you may need to go 'foraging' in your local greengrocer or supermarket.

Separate the egg whites carefully from the yolks (use the yolks to beef up your scrambled egg for breakfast) and then whip the whites in a glass bowl, gradually adding the caster sugar. You can add your choice of flavouring, syrup, or vanilla essence at this point if you like.

When the meringue mixture has reached the perfect consistency (Nigella and Delia talk about 'soft peaks'), spoon it on to the prepared baking tray (you can also use cupcake moulds, ramekins, or your receptacle of choice) and flatten out a hollow in each meringue for the fruit to sit in.

Put the tray in the preheated oven to bake for 1 hour 20 minutes, or a little longer if you like your meringue crispy. Allow your meringues to cool completely once baked. Some people like to turn off the oven and leave them there, though you can transfer them to a wire rack for cooling.

Bring your berries out of the freezer, allowing them to thaw and 'mush' a little before placing them on top of your meringues, filling the hollows you created, just before you're ready to serve them.

A shake of icing sugar (through a sieve of course) and a sprig of mint will make the mother-in-law think you studied at Ballymaloe.

WILLOWBROOK FARM

· ·

BY DR LUTFI

"Among the many benefits of adopting a sustainable farming lifestyle was rediscovering the abundance and diversity of produce, and the pleasures of preparing food with fresh ingredients from our own garden."

Willowbrook Farm grew out of our desire to create a space where we could live as a family in harmony with nature, somewhere we could rear and grow healthy, wholesome and nutritious food. We strive to farm ethically and sustainably and to live in tune with nature and the seasons. Having come from academic backgrounds, we had no practical farming skills and this meant a steep learning curve in the early years. We also had very limited financial means and had only been able to buy empty farmland. However, we saw its potential and embraced living rough in caravans until we could afford to self-build our first timber building. Now the farm is home to hens, sheep, goats, alpaca and ducks as well as a large vegetable garden, woodland and a fruit and nut orchard.

We felt that it wasn't enough to simply farm the land organically if our personal lives relied on the use of unsustainable materials. So, our energy comes from wind and solar power to the bio-mass boiler system which is fuelled by sustainable timber from the 6,000 trees we have planted on the farm over the last 20 years. On the farm itself, most of the energy required is good old-fashioned manual labour from the Willowbrook Farmers: Ruby and myself along with our five children, two daughters-in-law and two grandchildren who are happy to accompany me around the farm collecting eggs and keeping an eye on things. We also employ four local farm workers and welcome various volunteers through the WWOOF scheme, which creates a communal, social environment that we believe is crucial to the success of sustainable farming.

Over the years we have witnessed the growth of our farm business as well as the natural regeneration of the land. Woodlands planted almost twenty years ago have become home to diverse multi-layered ecosystems, hedgerows have been reinstated and pollinators introduced alongside a flourishing orchard and vegetable garden. We have also maintained our important role as educators by regularly opening our farm to our customers and visitors, hosting events and even an annual rural arts and music festival. Having come into farming from minority ethnic backgrounds and experienced incidents and issues of racism and exclusion in farming, part of our role has been to raise this topic in different forums. Among the many benefits of adopting a sustainable farming lifestyle was rediscovering the abundance and diversity of produce, and the pleasures of preparing food with fresh ingredients from our own garden.

CHICKEN WITH YOGHURT AND CASHEW NUTS

. . . .

Before serving this delicious dish, scatter fresh chopped coriander and ginger cut into fine matchsticks over the top for an extra burst of flavour. It's even better served alongside fresh crusty bread and a green salad. Recipe by Ghazala Agostini.

2 tbsp olive oil

2 tbsp black mustard seeds

1-1.5kg chicken, skinned and cut into small pieces

1 tsp each of garlic and ginger paste

1 medium-size onion, chopped

½ tsp ground turmeric

1 tsp chilli powder

Salt, to taste

8 tbsp Greek yoghurt

80ml water

100g cashew nuts, ground

Heat the oil in a wide, heavy-based pan and then add the mustard seeds. When they change colour and begin to pop, lay the chicken pieces into the pan and cook, turning occasionally, for about 5 minutes on a high heat.

Now lower the heat to medium and add the garlic, ginger and onion to the pan. Continue cooking, turning occasionally, for a further 3-4 minutes.

Next, add the turmeric, chilli powder and salt. Cook the spices, turning occasionally, for 2 minutes before stirring in the yoghurt and water. Cover the pan with a lid and simmer until the chicken is cooked through.

Lastly, add the ground cashews and mix well. At this point, adjust the seasoning if required and simmer for 5 minutes before serving.

PREPARATION TIME: 20 MINUTES | COOKING TIME: 30-40 MINUTES | SERVES 6

WOOD FARM
FREE RANGE EGGS LTD

· ·

BY CHARLES MEAR

"The feedback we get from customers makes me feel ten feet tall; it makes all the tough times you get with farming worthwhile."

Wood Farm has been in my family since 1948, so Jo and I were thrilled to have the opportunity to buy it in 2012, making us the fourth generation of farmers. In 1996, my dad and I took the plunge and decided to try free-range egg production. After a few teething problems, things soon settled down and I have never looked back. Jo left London and joined the farm in 2003. She found my enthusiasm for the farm and the hens contagious, so we decided to create our own brand and sell our eggs direct. The feedback we get from customers makes me feel ten feet tall; it makes all the tough times you get with farming worthwhile. We are passionate about our free-range hens and their eggs but also about the environment, which is why we looked into pioneering ways to become carbon neutral.

In our efforts to be as green as possible, we mill our feed for the hens on the farm using solar energy. We use wheat and barley from neighbouring farmers and add vitamins, nutrients, probiotics and enriched natural yeasts to keep the hens at the peak of health. In 2019 we met the Better Origin team and started to feed black soldier fly larvae (BSFL insect protein) to the hens in the first experiment of its kind worldwide to try and reduce our reliance on imported soya. We continue to work with Better Origin on a commercial basis to see if we can feed the hens a soy-free diet utilising homegrown proteins in conjunction with the BSFL.

In 2016 we built a farm-scale, crop-fed Anaerobic Digester (AD) to produce more green electricity, fuelled by home-grown maize and rye. Around 10% of this electricity is needed to power the farm, the rest is exported to power approximately 340 local homes. The heat from this process dries the chicken manure (capturing the ammonia with a biological air scrubber) and our matured digestate, turning it into a nutrient-rich, lightweight soil conditioner. We use these products to add organic matter and nutrients into our own soil and drive the yields of next year's crops, as well as selling to local folk and retail outlets. This circular farming is why we called our latest venture Full Circle Growing.

Farm life is busy, especially with three children, but the whole family realised the benefits of it during recent lockdowns. Days off are few and far between but being able to pop in and spend time with the children makes it all worth it.

CRÈME BRULÉE

· ·

This is a family favourite and of course uses Wood Farm's free-range eggs! A great friend of ours who amazingly made all the food for our wedding passed this recipe on to me. I like to use medium eggs as the yolk size is the same as a large egg.

6 eggs (I tend to use medium)

½ tsp vanilla essence

2 tbsp caster sugar, plus extra for sprinkling on top

1 pint (568ml) double cream

1 punnet of fresh raspberries

Separate the eggs and put the yolks in a bowl, reserving the whites for another recipe. Mix the yolks with a fork (not a whisk) and then stir in the vanilla essence and sugar.

Meanwhile, heat the cream in a saucepan but do not let it boil. Once hot, take the pan off the heat and stir the cream into the egg mixture until combined.

Firmly tap the bowl on a flat surface a few times to remove any air bubbles in the mixture. Pour equal amounts into 6 ramekins (no more than three quarters full) and cook at 180°c in a bain-marie for 25 minutes. What this means is to place the ramekins in a deep roasting tin large enough to hold all 6 of them without touching each other, then pour freshly boiled water into the tin (being careful not to splash the brulées) until it reaches halfway up the ramekins. Place the bain-marie carefully into the preheated oven and cook for the specified time.

Once the brulées are cooked, remove the ramekins from the bain-marie and allow to cool, then cover and place in the fridge for at least 2 hours but preferably 6 hours or longer.

20 minutes before you want to serve, sprinkle each brulée with a thin layer of caster sugar and either use a cook's blowtorch or a hot grill to melt the sugar until it has turned dark gold. Leave for 5 minutes for the sugar to set into a crisp topping, then serve with a few raspberries on the side. Yum!

PREPARATION TIME: 10 MINUTES, PLUS AT LEAST 2 HOURS CHILLING | COOKING TIME: 40 MINUTES | SERVES 6

WRIGHT FARM PRODUCE

BY KATHRYN WRIGHT

"Being in the agricultural and specifically the horticultural industry is so much more than just growing food; it is engineering, computerisation, agronomy, harvesting, marketing, problem solving. In short, it is about the people within it."

Wright Farm Produce is a producer of salad crops – namely iceberg lettuce, Little Gem lettuce, celery and Chinese leaves – based in West Lancashire. The business as it is today was established in 2008 but has a long family history stretching back through many generations of arable, horticultural, field vegetables, root crops and livestock farmers.

The crops we grow today are well suited to the highly productive peat soils in our area. We conventionally grow salad crops for several outlets, retailers, wholesalers and processors. The natural resources we have are our greatest asset and enable us to grow the crops we do, which are all harvested by hand, packed in the field and distributed the same day to make sure they are the freshest they can be when they reach the consumer.

Being in the agricultural and specifically the horticultural industry is so much more than just growing food; it is engineering, computerisation, agronomy, harvesting, marketing, problem solving. In short, it is about the people within it. As a horticultural business, we are judged by the crops we grow and as owners we are rightly proud of the produce we put on the shelf. However, we are just a small part of a much bigger industry and without all the links in the chain and the interactions between us all, we would not be able to attain the levels we do.

We are very fortunate to have some of the best people on our team of staff; they put in incredible effort in all conditions to help us provide top quality produce for our customers and consumers, who challenge us daily to meet a specific set of standards. We also work with suppliers, incredible businesses and individuals without whose knowledge, skills and support we would find it impossible to keep producing every single day.

I am incredibly lucky to be able to do a job that I enjoy, and of course there are days when you wonder how you are going to overcome an issue or wonder why you are doing it at all, but these days are far and away overshadowed by the pride in the quality crops we produce and the long-standing interactions and relationships with our customers, suppliers and employees, all of whom play an essential role in enabling Wright Farm Produce to continue.

SWEET AND SOUR CHINESE LEAVES

···

This recipe was chosen as there is an increasing interest in Oriental cooking. By using a limited number of ingredients, this recipe allows the Chinese leaves to be the main focus of the dish. Chinese leaves are a really versatile product as they can be eaten raw in salads but also cooked in stir fries.

1 head of Chinese leaf

1 hot red chilli pepper

2 tbsp soy sauce

2 tbsp vinegar

1 ½ tbsp honey

1 tbsp cornflour

1 tbsp sesame oil

1 tbsp olive oil

1 tbsp miso paste

Slice the Chinese leaf into strips. Cut open the red chilli and remove the seeds, then slice into small rings. Set the prepared Chinese leaves and red chilli to one side.

In a small bowl, combine the soy sauce, vinegar and honey before stirring in the cornflour. When that has dissolved, stir in the sesame oil and then set the sauce to one side.

Heat the olive oil in a wok or large frying pan over a moderate heat, then add the sliced chilli and miso paste. Stir fry for a few seconds, then add the Chinese leaves.

Stir fry for another 2-3 minutes until the Chinese leaves begin to soften, then add the soy and honey sauce. Cook for a further 2 minutes until the Chinese leaves begin to glaze. Serve immediately.

PREPARATION TIME: 15 MINUTES | COOKING TIME: 5-10 MINUTES | SERVES 2 OR 4 AS A SIDE DISH

YEO VALLEY ORGANIC

BY TIM MEAD

"Our desire to accelerate organic food into the nation's diets by making it accessible and readily available has not waned. If anything, we're redoubling our efforts to help people better understand the benefits of food produced from regenerative organic farming systems like ours."

Our journey began over 60 years ago in Somerset's Yeo Valley, when my parents bought Holt Farm and a herd of 30 British Friesian cows in 1961. Back then we were farming in a way that didn't have a label. It was about working in harmony with our environment and my family has been doing it since the 15th century. The land at Holt Farm was wet, rich in grass species and good for dairy cows. During the 1970s we started making yoghurt with leftover skimmed milk from the tearooms, which was still quite exotic then. In the 1990s, we decided to produce organic yoghurt and work with a cooperative of British organic dairy farmers who would supply Yeo Valley, with a guarantee to buy their milk to meet our growing demand. Fast forward to today and we use over 100 million litres of organic milk a year and sell two million products a week, supporting over 100 British organic dairy farmers.

I'm still very much the farming apprentice; my mother is the farmer of the family, now joined by my nephew. She has championed sustainable dairy farming for the past 60 years and is a firm believer in farming forever. Pedigree British Friesian cows are her lifelong passion and the Lakemead herd has earned her the reputation as one of the finest breeders in the country. We remain a family business and our production company is now 20% employee-owned.

Our desire to accelerate organic food into the nation's diets by making it accessible and readily available has not waned. If anything, we're redoubling our efforts to help people better understand the benefits of food produced from regenerative organic farming systems like ours. Across our farms in the Yeo Valley and on the Mendip Hills, our dairy, beef cattle and sheep are helping to regenerate soil, locking in carbon and helping to reverse climate change. Our grazing ground is holistically managed, and chemical-free. We've measured the carbon in the soil on our own farm and found that we have equivalent to 150 years' worth of the farm's annual emissions. Now we're expanding soil measuring and mentoring across our supplying farms. We see our role as twofold, firstly to provide natural healthy food and secondly to do so in a way that puts more back into the land than we take out.

HERBY BEEF WELLINGTON
WITH CHIMICHURRI BUTTER

There's no better way to celebrate a delicious piece of beef than in a Wellington, and we've given this one a twist. It's worth getting the best meat you can; we love to know where our meat is from and we're lucky to have our own organic grass-fed mob grazed beef cattle.

For the Wellington

Olive oil

1kg fillet of beef

Yeo Valley Organic unsalted butter

1 pack of ready-rolled puff pastry

8 slices of Parma ham

1 tbsp chopped fresh parsley

1 tbsp chopped fresh coriander

1 free-range egg

1 tbsp Yeo Valley Organic milk

For the chimichurri butter

1 block of Yeo Valley Organic unsalted butter, at room temperature

½ small bunch each of fresh coriander, parsley and thyme

2 cloves of garlic, peeled

1 tsp chilli flakes

Salt, to taste

For the Wellington

Heat a generous drizzle of olive oil in a large frying pan on a high heat and sear the beef all over. Add a large knob of butter and baste the beef once melted. Leave the seared beef fillet in the fridge to cool while you prepare the rest of the ingredients.

Place the ready-rolled pastry on a floured surface and gently roll it slightly bigger. Lay the slices of Parma ham on the pastry with the edges slightly overlapping, leaving a border around the edge. Sprinkle the herbs on top, then lay the beef fillet in the centre.

Beat the egg with the milk in a small bowl and use this to brush the uncovered pastry. Fold the pastry over the beef and then roll it over until you get a seam at the base of the Wellington. Tuck the sides under and then brush the pastry with more egg wash to coat all over. Chill the Wellington in the fridge for at least an hour, or even overnight.

For the chimichurri butter

Combine all the ingredients in a blender, adding more or less chilli depending on your heat preference! Roll the butter into a sausage shape using a sheet of cling film, then chill in the fridge for at least an hour.

To cook the Wellington, preheat the oven to 200°c and transfer it straight from the fridge to a baking tray, then place in the hot oven to cook for 30-35 minutes. Leave the Wellington to rest for at least 15 minutes once done, then serve with slices of the chimichurri butter, your favourite salad and roasted beetroots.

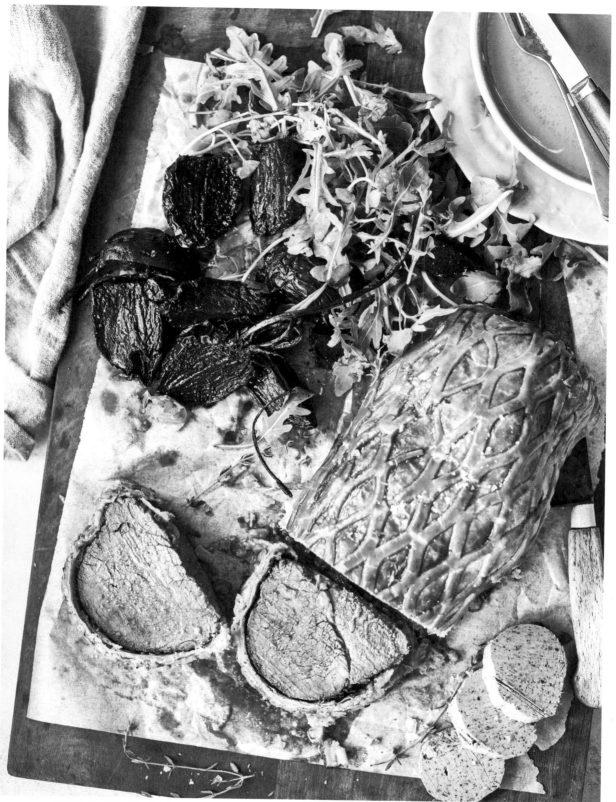

PREPARATION TIME: 30 MINUTES, PLUS AT LEAST 1 HOUR CHILLING | COOKING TIME: 35 MINUTES | SERVES 8

DIRECTORY

Abi Reader

Find me on Twitter @AbiReader and
Instagram @AbiReader1

*I work a traditional mixed farm in South Wales, milking cows,
rearing Welsh beef and lamb and growing a few crops to try and
be self-sufficient in the livestock feed and bedding we use.*

Balcaskie Estate

Easter Kellie Farm, Arncroach, Anstruther, Fife KY10 2RF
Telephone: 01333 720200
Email: info@balcaskie.com
Website: www.balcaskie.com
Facebook: @BalcaskieEstate
Find us on Instagram @balcaskie_estate
and Twitter @Balcaskie

*A modern working estate in East Fife committed to cultivating
and caring for the natural environment, nurturing local business,
and supporting our vibrant community.*

Belvoir Farm Drinks Ltd

Barkestone Lane, Bottesford, Leicestershire NG13 0DH
Telephone: 01476 870286
Email: pev@belvoirfarm.co.uk
Website: www.belvoirfarm.co.uk
Facebook: belvoirfarm
Find us on Instagram @belvoirfarm_uk

*At Belvoir Farm we make soft drinks from masses of the best
ingredients such as real fruits, flowers, and spices for delicious
natural tastes with absolutely nothing bad: Crafted with Nature.*

**Bread for Good Community Benefit Society
Trading as Scotland The Bread**

Unit 8 The Bowhouse, St. Monan's, Anstruther, Fife
KY10 2FB
Telephone: 01333 730625
Email: info@scotlandthebread.org
Website: www.scotlandthebread.org
Facebook: ScotlandTheBread
Find us on Instagram @scotlandthebread and
Twitter @scotlandbread

*A collaborative project to grow better grain and bake better
bread with the common purposes of nourishment, sustainability
and food justice.*

The Buffalo Farm Limited

Boglily Farm Steading, Boglily Road, Fife KY2 5XY
Telephone: 01592 646252
Email: orders@thebuffalofarm.co.uk
Website: www.thebuffalofarm.co.uk
Facebook: The Buffalo Farm
Find us on Instagram @the.buffalofarm

*Fife's leading farm shop and Scotland's only producer of prime
buffalo mozzarella. From field to fork, there's no other farm quite
like it.*

The Bull Inn

Rotherfold Square, Little Totnes, Totnes, TQ9 5SN
Telephone: 01803 640040
Website: www.bullinntotnes.co.uk
Email: office@bullinntotnes.co.uk
Find us on Instagram @bullinn_totnes

*The Bull Inn is an organic, radically ethical pub owned by Geetie
Singh Watson. Ingredient-led dishes, cooked from scratch and
honestly sourced from likeminded suppliers. Follow our No-Bull
Rules.*

Colwith Farm Potatoes

Colwith Farm, Par, Cornwall PL24 2TU
Telephone: 07500 872639
Website: www.colwithfarm.co.uk
Email: hello@colwithfarm.co.uk
Find us on Facebook and Instagram @colwithfarm

*Fifth generation premium quality potato growers based in mid
Cornwall. Growing for a variety of sectors including home use,
crisps, chips, and of course the Cornish pasty!*

Clougher Farm

9 Clougher Road, Bushmills, Co. Antrim, Northern Ireland
BT57 8XP
Telephone: 07710 940 458
Email: v.chestnutt@btinternet.com
Facebook: Clougherfarm
Find us on Instagram @Clougher_farm

*Family farm producing dairy, beef and sheep including pedigree
breeds for breeding and commercial use, based in Bushmills on
the beautiful North Antrim coast.*

Droitwich Salt

Churchfields Saltworks, Salwarpe, Droitwich Spa, Worcestershire, WR9 0AH
Telephone: 01905 451289
Email: info@droitwichsalt.com
Facebook: droitwichsalt
Find us on Instagram and Twitter @droitwich_salt

Churchfields Saltworks are proud to be the new custodians of Droitwich Salt, reviving this natural, ancient and pure resource after 100 years.

E. Oldroyd & Sons (Lofthouse) Ltd

Hopefield Farm, The Shutts, Leadwell Lane, Rothwell, Leeds LS26 0ST
Telephone: 0113 282 2245
Email: visits@eoldroyd.co.uk
Website: www.yorkshireforcedrhubarb.co.uk

Producers and packers of quality rhubarb and strawberries.

EWE MATTER (Woodbury Ryelands)

Old Woodbury Farmhouse, Drove Road, Gamlingay, Sandy, Bedfordshire SG19 2HS
Telephone: 07887 753324
Email: whalegreensimmentals@gmail.com

Breeding, neutering and supplying British native lamb direct to our customers' table.

The Farmer's Son

Clentrie Farm, Auchtertool KY2 5XG
Telephone: 0131 463 8123
Email: info@thefarmersson.com
Website: www.thefarmersson.com
Find us on social media @thefarmerssonuk

Based in the beautiful countryside of Fife, we use the finest all-natural Scottish ingredients to produce our award-winning artisanal haggis, black pudding, white pudding and Lorne sausage.

Farm Wilder

Elston Farm, Copplestone, Crediton, EX17 5PB
Telephone: 01363 84545
Website: www.farmwilder.co.uk
Email: shop@farmwilder.co.uk
Find us on social media @farmwilder

Farm Wilder works in harmony with nature, creating wonderful meat boxes while changing how we farm to benefit animals, farmers, consumers, wildlife and the natural world.

Farrington's Mellow Yellow

Bottom Farm, Brook Street, Hargrave, Wellingborough, Northamptonshire NN9 6BP
Telephone: 01933 622809
Email: info@farrington-oils.co.uk
Website: www.farrington-oils.co.uk
Find us on Facebook and Instagram @MellowYellowKitchen or Twitter @RapeseedOilFans

Farrington's Mellow Yellow produce carbon and plastic neutral cold pressed rapeseed oil and salad dressings on their farm in Northamptonshire to sustainable LEAF (Linking Environment And Farming) Marque standards.

F B Parrish and Son Ltd

Lodge Farm, Chicksands, Shefford, Bedfordshire SG17 5QB
Telephone: 01462 813260
Email: support@parrishfarms.co.uk
Website: www.parrishfarms.co.uk
Facebook: FBParrish

F B Parrish and Son is a third generation, family-run arable farm offering UK-grown, premium quality onions and shallots.

Forest Fungi

The Shroom Rooms, Warren Road, Dawlish Warren, Devon EX7 0NG
Telephone: 01626 864111
Email: scott@forestfungi.co.uk
Website: www.forestfungi.co.uk

Forest Fungi are growers of organic gourmet mushrooms with an onsite farm shop, café, and visitor centre.

Glass Brothers

Website: www.glassbrothers.co.uk
Find us on LinkedIn @GlassBrothers

Northern Irish manufacturer of Bramley apple products, nurturing our food from tree to customer.

Goodwood

Chichester, West Sussex PO18 0PH
Telephone: 01243 755000
Email: media@goodwood.com
Website: goodwood.com
Find us on Instagram @goodwood

Goodwood is England's greatest sporting estate. Seat of the Dukes of Richmond since 1697, the family has always welcomed their friends and guests to share in their love of sport.

The Gourmet Goat Farmer Ltd

East Farm, Winterbourne Monkton, Swindon,
Wiltshire SN4 9NW
Telephone: 01672 539510
Email: hello@thegourmetgoatfarmer.co.uk
Website: www.thegourmetgoatfarmer.co.uk
Find us on social media @thegourmetgoatfarmer

With a passion for all things goat, we bring together conservation and collaboration to increase the biodiversity on our farm and showcase the very best of British goat produce.

Heather Hills Farm

Bridge of Cally, Blairgowrie, Perthshire PH10 7JG
Telephone: 01250 886252
Email: info@heatherhills.co.uk
Website: www.heatherhills.co.uk
Find us on Facebook and Twitter @heatherhillsuk

One of Scotland's leading producers of award-winning artisan honeys and preserves, championed for their superior provenance, quality and flavour.

Holkham

Holkham Hall, Wells-next-the-Sea, Norfolk NR23 1AB
Telephone: 01328 710227
Website: www.holkham.co.uk
Email: enquiries@holkham.co.uk
Find us on social media @holkhamestate

The stunning coastal landscape, magnificent stately home, rolling parkland, attractions and events make Holkham a wonderful place to visit. It's also a thriving, pioneering and sustainable rural estate.

Hugh Lowe Farms Ltd

Barons Place, Mereworth, Maidstone, Kent ME18 5NF
Telephone: 01622 812229
Email: info@hlf.co.uk
Website: www.hughlowefarms.co.uk
Find us on LinkedIn @hugh-lowe-farms-limited and Instagram @hughlowefarms

A fifth-generation family-owned berry farm in Kent, headed by Marion Regan, known for our people, innovation and quality.

Humble by Nature

Upper Meend Farm, Monmouth, NP25 4RP
Telephone: 01600 714595
Email: info@humblebynature.com
Website: www.humblebynature.com
Facebook: humblebynature
Find us on Twitter and Instagram @farmerhumble

Humble by Nature is home to a busy working farm, a thriving rural skills centre with a wide range of courses and events, and delightful holiday accommodation.

Jekka's

Shellards Lane, Alveston, Bristol BS35 3SY
Telephone: 01454 418878
Email: sales@jekkas.com
Website: www.jekkas.com
Find us on social media @jekkasherbfarm

Jekka's is a family-run herb farm in the UK with over 35 years' experience in growing and using medicinal and culinary herb plants and seeds.

Jimmy's Farm & Wildlife Park
Pannington Hall Lane, Wherstead, Ipswich IP9 2AP
Telephone: 01473 604206
Email: enquiries@jimmysfarm.com
Website: www.jimmysfarm.com
Facebook: Jimmy Doherty
Find us on Instagram & Twitter @jimmysfarm

As seen on TV, we are home to over 80 different species and breeds! We are a working farm and wildlife park open for visitors seven days a week.

The Little White Lamb Co. Ltd
Trading as ECOEWE
3 Grigsons Wood, East Harling, Norwich,
Norfolk NR16 2LW
Telephone: 07759574647
Email: info@ecoewe.co.uk
Find us on Facebook and Instagram @ecoewe

Purveyors of award-winning lamb, putting provenance and welfare at the heart of our business.

Person & Freire Ltd
Paeony Cottage, Les Charrieres Nicolle, St. Lawrence,
Jersey CI, JE3 1HJ
Telephone: 07797711581
Email: personfreire@gmail.com
Facebook: Joefreirejerseystrawberries

Locally grown fruit, veg and flowers including strawberries, raspberries, asparagus, paeonies and many more.

Knepp Wild Range
The Estate Office, Knepp Castle, West Grinstead, West
Sussex RH13 8LJ
Telephone: 01403 915750
Email: wildrange@knepp.co.uk
Website: www.kneppwildrangemeat.co.uk
Facebook: Kneppwildrangemeat
Find us on Instagram @kneppwildrangemeat

In our rewilding project, free-roaming animals live outside all year round in natural herds, making a positive contribution to nature and carbon capture. The wide variety of herbs, grasses and leafy vegetation they browse on means they are superbly healthy and the meat is good for us too.

L'Enclume
Cavendish Street, Cartmel, Cumbria LA11 6QA
Telephone: 015395 36362
Email: info@lenclume.co.uk
Website: www.lenclume.co.uk
Facebook: lenclumerestaurant
Find us on Twitter and Instagram @lenclume

L'Enclume is Simon Rogan's flagship restaurant, in the Lake District village of Cartmel. Known for its seasonal farm-to-table philosophy and use of hyper-seasonal produce.

Malt Coast Brewery
Branthill Farm, Wells next the Sea, Norfolk NR23 1SB
Telephone: 07881378900
Email: info@maltcoast.com
Website: www.maltcoast.com
Find us on social media @maltcoast

A craft brewery brewing beers with a focus on provenance using our own farm's malting barley. A genuine grain to glass story.

Millbank Farm
11 Mill Road, Killinchy BT23 6PG
Telephone: 07593 922906
Millbank Farm Shop LTD
30 Main Street, Saintfield BT24 7AA
Telephone: 028 97512692
Email: emily@millbankfarm.com
Website: www.millbankfarm.com
Find us on Instagram and Facebook @millbankfarm

Medium mixed farm of 400 acres established in 1889. The farm produces lamb, poultry, vegetables and sells its produce in Millbank Farm Shop, the farm's first direct-to-consumer business in Saintfield.

One Girl and Her Cows

Website: onegirlandhercows.co.uk
Email: onegirlandhercows@gmail.com
Facebook: One Girl and Her Cows
Find me on Instagram @onegirlandhercows

Blogging from our Yorkshire farm, covering everything from farming to faulty health, and my journey with both, while trying to bring a bit of the countryside to others.

Riverford Organic Farmers

Wash Barn, Buckfastleigh, Devon TQ11 0JU
Telephone: 01803 227227
Email: help@riverford.co.uk
Website: www.riverford.co.uk
Find us on social media @riverford

Riverford is an employee-owned ethical business that grows and delivers organic produce; our mission is to inspire people to cook with amazing veg that makes a positive impact.

Shimpling Park Farms Limited

Shimpling, Bury St Edmunds, Suffolk IP29 4HY
Telephone: 01284 827317
Email: info@shimplingparkfarms.com
Website: www.shimplingpark.com
Find us on social media @ShimplingPark

We farm in a way that enhances nature, improves our soils, loves our animals and keeps us and those that we work with healthy and happy!

Sitopia Farm

331 Shooters Hill, London DA16 3RP
Email: hello@sitopiafarm.com
Website: www.sitopiafarm.com
Find us on Instagram and Twitter @sitopiafarm

A modern urban farm in London growing vegetables, salads, fruit, herbs and flowers using regenerative agricultural techniques and selling locally.

Springhill Farms (Pershore) Ltd
Trading as EVG Europe

Birmingham Road, Blackminster, Evesham, Worcestershire WR11 7TD
Telephone: 01386 830967
Email: info@evgltd.co.uk
Website: www.evgltd.co.uk
Facebook: Evesham Vale Growers
Find us on Twitter, Instagram, LinkedIn and TikTok @evg_europe

Growers of premium tomatoes, salad crops, and forage crops in Worcestershire and beyond, all while producing as sustainably as possible.

Village Farm

Website: www.villagefarm.org.uk

We champion local British farm produce and are passionate about showing people what happens on the other side of the farm gate.

Willowbrook Farm

Hampton Gay, Oxfordshire OX5 2QQ
Email: enquiries@willowbrookfarm.co.uk
Website: www.willowbrookfarm.co.uk
Facebook: Willowbrook.Farm.Oxford
Find us on Instagram @willowbrookfarmers and Twitter @willowbrook_org

A vibrant family farm in Oxfordshire based on principles of responsible stewardship and social and environmental sustainability.

Wood Farm Free Range Eggs

Wood Farm, Vicarage Road, Warelsy, Near Sandy, Bedfordshire SG19 3DA
Telephone: 07850 630777
Email: jo@woodfarmfreerangeeggs.co.uk
Facebook: Wood Farm Free Range Eggs Ltd
Instagram: @woodfarmfreerangeeggs
Twitter: @WoodEggs

Free-range eggs, green electricity and soil conditioner farmers.

Wright Farm Produce

Rutland, Taylors Meanygate, Tarleton, Preston, Lancashire
PR4 6XB
Telephone: 01772 812704
Email: office@wrightfarmproduce.co.uk
Website: www.wrightfarmproduce.co.uk
Facebook: Wright Farm Produce

*Producer and supplier of quality salad crops to the retail,
wholesale and catering sectors, taking pride in our growing and
production techniques.*

Yeo Valley Organic

Yeo Valley HQ, Rhodyate, Blagdon BS40 7YE
Telephone: 01761 462 798
Email: hello@yeovalley.co.uk
Website: www.yeovalley.co.uk
Find us on social media @yeovalley

Britain's largest organic dairy brand, established in 1994.

OTHER TITLES IN THIS SERIES

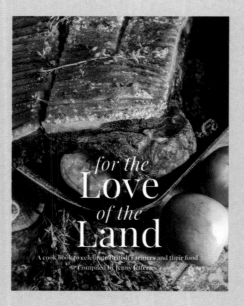

This is a cook book to celebrate British farming in all its hardship and glory. For many families, working the land and raising livestock is a true labour of love, and what they produce is the backbone of the country's food and drink. The dishes in this book make the most of local and seasonal ingredients, creating delicious meals, puddings and bakes that anyone can cook up at home. Alongside that, members of these farming families have told the stories of their livelihoods: from losing sheep in snowstorms to stoking enthusiasm in the next generation, their honesty and passion is an inspiration and an education. Recipes include Blackbrook Beef Bolognese from a traditional lowland farm in Leicestershire, Reestit Mutton Soup by two sisters who run their family farm on Shetland and Pheasant and Asparagus Crumble by game farmers from Cambridgeshire, as well as Kentish Lavender Shortbread from Castle Farm and a cocktail featuring fresh edible flowers from Greens of Devon. As the landscape of British farming changes, we need to support high-quality food production and understand how farmers can work in harmony with nature to make our eating habits more sustainable. Whether you're country born and bred or have never donned a pair of wellies, discover the food and stories in this book to help put British farming back on the map and at the centre of your table.

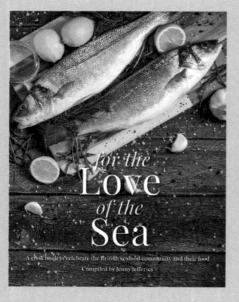

Following the success of For The Love of the Land, this second cook book compiled by Jenny Jefferies and produced by Meze Publishing showcases the incredible fish and seafood found in the UK. For The Love of the Sea highlights the hard work and dedication of the men and women who work in the British fishing industry, as well as those who support them such as the Royal National Lifeboat Institution. The book features professional sailors, fishmongers, fishermen and women, marine conservationists, chefs and suppliers, as well as a foreword by Marcus Coleman, the Chief Executive of Seafish which works with businesses and the government to support the UK seafood sector. With over 40 delicious recipes and fascinating stories from the contributors, For The Love of the Sea aims to encourage everyone to fall in love with British fish and seafood again, championing sustainability and celebrating great produce.

AVAILABLE FROM GOOD BOOK SHOPS, OR ONLINE AT WWW.MEZEPUBLISHING.CO.UK